Father Forgive Them for They Know Not What They Do

Other Books by the Author

Unseen Love

*Unseen Love i*s a mysterious love story that captures the imagination and challenges the reader to discover the seen but unseen within the novel. www.unseenlove.com

Hidden Away

Is a suspense that keeps the reader wondering what hidden away covert actions are happening in Big Stone Gap, a small Southwest Virginia town in the Appalachian Mountains.

God in Mathematics the Novel

Does mathematics define an Omni present entity that really is nothing? Could this be taken to show that God is nothing? Find out in God in Mathematics the novel.

Baby Power

Do babies think, plan and eavesdrop on their outside surroundings in the womb? Discover how one did and how his plans went awry. In doing so you might relive some of your growing years.

Why are we here? From where did we come? Answered

Ever wondered about the soul's origin? Discover the three concepts and weigh them against Christianity's views. You might come away surprised.

Father Forgive Them for They Know Not What They Do

Arthur L. Saxton
Lousville KY

Studio of Books LLC
5900 Balcones Drive Suite 100
Austin, Texas 78731
www.studioofbooks.org
Hotline: (254) 800-1183

Ordering Information:
Special discounts are available on quantity purchases by corporations, associations, and others. For details, contact the publisher at the address above.

Printed in the United States of America.

ISBN-13:   Softcover   978-1-964928-52-4
           eBook   978-1-964928-53-1

Library of Congress Control Number:

DEDICATION

To my parents John and Alice Saxton, a coal miner and housewife, I dedicate this book. With little formal education, they provided my brother and me with the highest form of education available. They taught us how to love unconditionally through the simple but powerful concept they called the Golden Rule of Life "Do unto others as you would have them to do unto you."

Thanks Mama & Daddy

TABLE *of* CONTENTS

ACKNOWLEDGEMENTS

I thank my wife, Genella Saxton, for taking the time to proofread this book and questioning areas that were not clear and offering suggestions for improvement. I will always be indebted to her for her constructive critical proofing and catching many of the errors that I overlooked in my several readings for errors after completing the book.

FROM THE AUTHOR

The main purpose of this book is to examine the meaning of the statement that Christ made on the cross, *"Father, forgive them for they know not what they do."* I believe that the statement was not intended just for those involved in Christ's immediate crucifixion, but it was intended for all mankind. This book attempts to show the foundational teaching that God revealed to mankind about His plan of salvation for them. This is done by starting in Genesis and moving forward examining some of the familiar Bible stories in a more detailed manner, and pointing out God's teaching process.

In addition, I attempt to provide a logical reason for God's plan of salvation based on what I see as the main theme of the Bible. This theme is God's love for mankind's souls.

Based on this theme, I start with the possibility of souls existing with God before creation and use scripture to support my view. Using the same scripture, I establish that God loved us before creation. This love, I attempt to show, is why the plan of salvation was created. In addition the same verse that I use to establish the above points, I use to provide the reason Christ was on the cross justifying mankind.

As we move through the book from Genesis to the cross, other supporting information is provided indicating God's teaching and revealing His plan of salvation to mankind. What I hope the reader will take away from the read is that God love for our souls began before the creation of the world. He loved our souls so much that He wanted to provide souls with the ability to choose to spend eternity with Him instead of souls just existing there because they were created there. To this end, He created a temporary existence for them to make the choice of where they would spend eternity. If they chose to return to Him, then they would have a more abundant eternal life with Him than they did before, because they had the opportunity to experience and to understand how much God loved them, even when they did not deserve His love. Jesus speaks about a more abundant life for those saved by Him. *John 10:9-10 I am the door. If anyone enters by Me, he will be saved, and will go in and out and find pasture. The thief does not come except to steal, and to kill, and to destroy. I have come that they may have life, and that they may have it more abundantly.*

The lesson of how much God loved mankind was the lesson that He started teaching mankind from the beginning. The culmination of the lesson was Christ on the cross. *John 3:16 (NLT) "For this is how God loved the world: He gave his one and only Son, so that everyone who believes in him will not perish but have eternal life.*

My request is that you do not stop reading if you do not agree with some of the desired takeaway you just read. Read the book through to the end and then evaluate the contents. I am open to all comments and viewpoints.

Because I have taken some nontraditional views in interpreting some scripture verses, doubt has arisen in me at time about whether I should continue to write this book. The following verses have provided inspiration and have kept me going when doubt has arisen I questioned myself about continuing writing on this topic.

Encouragement to seek beyond the Accepted

Luke 11:9-13: "So I say to you: Ask and it will be given to you; seek and you will find; knock and the door will be opened to you. For everyone who asks receives; the one who seeks finds; and to the one who knocks, the door will be opened. "Which of you fathers, if your son asks for a fish, will give him a snake instead? Or if he asks for an egg, will give him a scorpion? If you then, though you are evil, know how to give good gifts to your children, how much more will your Father in heaven give the Holy Spirit to those who ask him!"

My Prayer For Spiritual Enlightenment, Guidance and Inspiration

Father I come asking that as I go about trying to write this book that you will open up my mind and endow me with your Holy Spirit that what comes from my mind will be inspired by you. Give me direction and guidance. Let me see the deeper meaning of your inspired word that I may share it as you lead me. Let me not insert my own prejudices and misguided thoughts in what I write as facts inspired by you but clearly state them as derived from me. If I fail in my efforts to convey your words and meaning as they were intended, I pray that you will still use them to turn someone toward you. I come humbly acknowledging my short comings and my failures, but I come asking for your grace and mercy to strengthen me where I am weak. In the name of Jesus Christ I pray. Amen

INTRODUCTION

There are so many things that occur in our lives that we do not understand. We often chalk them up as coincidence. I don't think they are and I hope when you finish this book, you will not also. God is active in our lives and I hope this book will help you see how He is and has been throughout mankind's beginning. If you don't believe that the Bible is divinely inspired by God, it's ok to doubt if you are truly searching for God's divine truth. I doubted it at one time, but it did not stop me from searching for the truth or God providing me with the answer. However, the only place the truth of the Bible can be found is by reading and searching it and asking for divine guidance in your search. One cannot rely totally on someone else's reading and interpretation of it. Each of us must read, ponder and rely on the Holy Spirit to provide the truth of it.

Some say don't question God because there are some thing He does not want us to know. If God doesn't want us to know something, He won't reveal it to us. I believe that God doesn't mind us questioning what we read in the Bible as long as we do not stop looking for the answers in His word. Don't take anyone's words, including what you read in this book as the absolute truth, but study and seek divine guidance. In doing so, remember that God gave you the gift of logic, so ask for His spiritual guidance in applying it to His word throughout your search.

As I reflect on my life and how God has led me to the point I have now reached, I marvel over it. Don't get me wrong and think that I believe that I have arrived at the pinnacle of where God desires me to be. I tell you that I have not and that I am so far from it. Yet, God's grace and mercy have brought me this far and has been teaching me as I earnestly search for His truth.

As I recall incidents in my life that I think are significant in regard to my spiritual growth to this point, I see the hand of God at work throughout my life. The thing that puzzles and amazes me the most is why God has included me among others to shower His mercy and grace upon. I know that I am not worthy of it, especially when some of the things that made and make me realize His grace the most were and are so far away from where He desires for me to be.

I remember accepting Christ into my life around the age of twelve years old. I basically did it because my parents told me that at the age of twelve my sins would no longer be on them but on me. They came to this point of view from the fact that at age twelve Jesus went to the temple listening and questioning the teachers. Luke 2:46 47: "After three days they found him in the temple courts, sitting among the teachers, listening to them and asking them questions. Everyone who heard him was amazed at his understanding and his answers." I gave my life to Christ and was baptized, but I really did not experience Christ and did not have a personal relationship with Him.

Somehow, I ended up going to Knoxville College in Knoxville TN, one of the historical black colleges. It was founded in 1875 by the United Presbyterian Church of North America. While attending, students were required to take a Bible course. After taking several Bible courses, my whole view of the Bible changed and by the time I left KC, I had a lot of questions about God. My parents, who were believers from their personal experiences and relationship with Christ, had instilled in me a view of God that the basic Bible courses destroyed. In my mind, when they said God wrote the Bible, I pictured that

He literally did. When I realized how the Bible came together and that some writings were left out of it, it took away the mystery and the divinity of it for me. I was caught between my parent's faith and belief, and my mind's rational reasoning. I could not reconcile the two and it left me trying to understand God's existence.

When I thought I was taking a semester break from school, and ended up drafted in the Army, my religious struggle did not end. It really increased. One of my friends was a young minister and he constantly talked to me about God. I constantly challenged him to prove God's existence to me. Of course, he always went to the Bible to do so. The problem with that for me was that my faith in the Bible as being God's word was shaken and I questioned the validity of the writing. We were finally separated and he failed to convince me about God. Of course, I had not completely stopped believing that God existed; I just couldn't come to completely accept it.

After leaving the military, I obtained a job with a company and for six years gave *two hundred percent* in effort to it. It was my first real job, and I had envisioned a career with the company. The company, a national credit corporation had placed most of its local business primarily with one company. A new district manager was appointed and tried to renegotiate a long standing contract with the company and the company pulled all of its accounts. The local branch of the credit corporation began to let people go. Although, I knew that my time would eventually come, I remained hoping against odds that I would weather the storm. I did not. Since I had given so much to the company, the loss of the job rattled and devastated my confidence in holding any job. I went into a state of depression and lingered around the house having a pity party. For some reason, I came to doubt if I was even thinking coherently and began talking into a tape recorder and listening to the play back trying to determine if I was thinking rationally.

My wife and I were living in an apartment which had sliding double mirror doors for the closet. She was at work and I was having my pity party at home alone. I walked passed the mirrors and looked into them. I heard a voice, but still don't know if it was aloud or inwardly, that said, "You can't do nothing without me." At that moment, I found myself standing in front of the mirror crying to Jesus, asking Him for His help. It was my first personal experience with Christ. Afterwards, I began to gradually change my attitude. From that first encounter, I have gradually come to know Him more personally, but still have a long way to go. I have had two other experiences through the years with His speaking to me and giving me audible or inward assurances. Each of these two times, I was worried and praying about a crisis in my life. After His assurance, I could no longer worry over the situations. One of the instances about which I was praying, could have destroyed my life and my family's life as we knew it. My wife and I were stressed over it until His assurance came to me. I did not know whether His assurance meant that the situation was going to be resolved as I desired or not, but I knew for sure that He said it was going to be okay. I only knew, the okay meant He was going to be with me through whatever the outcome was and it calmed me and brought peace to me as the crisis ran it course.

I also now know that God's word found in the Bible is His word. I know for sure it is divinely given. There is no more doubt for me. As I have been introduced more and more to His word, I see how it is made plain to those who really want to find the truth and proof of God's word. There is proof found in His word that His word is from an existence outside of our present reality of understanding. Already fulfilled prophecies are proofs; however, there are many more proofs that we will discuss that show the Bible as God's divine word. We will see how amazing they are. In addition to these, the fact that the different writings written centuries apart come together to tell the story of His Love and plan for mankind's eternity is divine in itself.

When I began writing this book, I had no intentions of sharing my journey. I don't even know why I am writing this book. I don't understand the motivation to do so. All I know is for some reason, I am doing it, and so I must believe it is inspired by God for me to do so. I wish I were more biblically knowledgeable to really drive home the different concepts that are touched on within this book. Since I am not, I must depend on insight from God for me to write whatever follows. I pray that you will be inspired in some manner to seek a closer relationship and to seek more knowledge about God and His plan for you. *Blessed reading!*

Chapter I

THE BEGINNING OF THE MEANING OF THE FORGIVENESS STATEMENT

Although the title of this book is, "Father Forgive them for they know not what they do" and the statement is found in the New Testament, we must go back to the beginning of the Old Testament to understand the true meaning of this statement. Many Christians have been led to believe that Christ's statement on the cross was directed toward the Roman soldiers who were there crucifying Him. However, I believe that the statement had a more far reaching meaning than that. As we progress through the book, I hope that I will be able to tell the story of its meaning so that it becomes clear that the statement's intent was not for those in Christ's immediacy but addressed the sin of the world. So, where did the beginning really begin in order to understand the story?

It began with God before He created the world. I mentioned above that we must go back to the Old Testament to understand Christ's statement on the cross. However, we must look to the New Testament to tell the story before God created the world. This may sound confusing but we will see what the Bible says about it as we progress and see if it also follows logic scripturally.

As we proceed we will pose questions and attempt to answer them scripturally in a logical spiritually led manner because I believe the Bible is the source we should seek to answer biblical questions which originate from the Bible. As I have learned more about the Bible, the more I have come to embrace this fact. So let's see what Scripture has to say that could lead me to make such a statement.

I will primarily use two Scriptures as a basis for the statement foundation and along the way; bring in other Scriptures to add more understanding. These two scriptures, one from the New Testament and one from the Old Testament, are Ephesians 1: 37 and Genesis 3:6 7, *Ephesians 1: 37 (NLT) All praise to God, the Father of our Lord Jesus Christ, who has blessed us with every spiritual blessing in the heavenly realms because we are united with Christ. Even before he made the world, God loved us and chose us in Christ to be holy and without fault in his eyes. God decided in advance to adopt us into his own family by bringing us to himself through Jesus Christ. This is what he wanted to do, and it gave him great pleasure. So we praise God for the glorious grace he has poured out on us who belong to his dear Son. He is so rich in kindness and grace that he purchased our freedom with the blood of his Son and forgave our sins.*

Genesis 3:67 "And when the woman saw that the tree was good for food, and that it was pleasant to the eyes, and a tree to be desired to make one wise, she took of the fruit thereof, and did eat, and gave also unto her husband with her; and he did eat. And the eyes of them both were opened, and they knew that they were naked; and they sewed fig leaves together, and made themselves aprons."

We will examine these two statements and see that they can be viewed as setting the main theme of the Bible from its beginning to its end. However the beginning or the end of the story may not be apparent to some. In Ephesians we see Paul explaining when, where and through whom God began providing us with His spiritual blessings. We also see what effect the spiritual blessing had on us. His spiritual blessing made us holy and blameless in God's sight. We also see what He planned for us at a later time through Jesus. He planned a closer relationship with us brought about through Christ; an adoption to son ship into His holy family.

In Genesis, we find the initiation of His plan and the promise of the adoption process which would occur through Christ through the reversal of Satan's act of removal of the holy and blameless state once possessed. As we travel through time to get to the cross, which is the end and also a new beginning, we must not forget the initial plan, and the creation story which laid the foundation to the cross. By keeping these seemingly two divergences in mind, we can keep our bearing and finally come to the convergence of the two divergences.

The Soul's Immortality

Before we begin on the journey to the cross and Christ's statement of forgiveness, we must address the controversy, that I recently discovered, that exists about the soul and its immortality. Because I grew up in a religious environment that always accepted the common belief that many Christians and other religions have that the soul is immortal, it never occurred to me that there is controversy about it among Christians. After I had almost completed writing this book, a friend of mine challenged me on the subject and presented seemingly convincing arguments against it. One of the arguments tied the existence of the concept of the immortal soul to Greek thinkers such as Plato and Origen. Another showed where the Hebrew word translated "soul" in the Old Testament is nephesh and means "a breathing creature." In addition to this, the friend referenced *Genesis 2:7 (KJV) And the Lord God formed man of the dust of the ground, and breathed into his nostrils the breath of life; and man became a living soul.*

From this reference and other scripture, the friend and apparently others, have concluded as proof that the word soul in scripture only refers to a mortal breathing being.

If this is the case then the word should never be used in the Old Testament to describe God since we know Christ told the woman at the well that God is spirit. *John 4:23-24 Yet a time is coming and has now come when the true worshipers will worship the Father in the Spirit and in truth, for they are the kind of worshipers the Father seeks. God is spirit, and his worshipers must worship in the Spirit and in truth."* In Judges 10:16 we find in the KJV the following. *And they put away the strange gods from among them, and served the Lord: and his soul was grieved for the misery of Israel.*

Here we find the word soul translated in reference to God. Since God is Spirit, then would not God's soul be spirit also?

We can gather that Christ was teaching the woman who God is and how God wants us to worship him. One of the main themes of this book is that God has been teaching mankind from the beginning about who He is and how He wants us to worship Him. One of the references my friend provided alluded to, in a scoffing manner, that some theologians have suggested that God had inspired the Greek thinkers to foster the idea of the soul's immortality. I believe that scripture shows that God has been teaching mankind about who He is since the beginning. As scripture also shows, He uses all of us to carry out His plan, even when we do not know it. A good example is Isaiah's prophecy about Cyrus the Great. See Isaiah 44: 24-28. We must remember that God made His plan of salvation even before He created the world. We really do not understand in depth why God created us and placed us here on earth. Could it be that His plan was to use mankind for a greater purpose than we realize? Could we be just a vessel for our souls to allow them to acquire a closer and more intimate relationship with Him by understanding His unfailing love for us through our break with Him? We will explore this possibility by looking at a nontraditional interpretation of one of the scriptures previously mentioned.

Since God is spirit, and since He created us in the image of Him by blowing the breath of life into us, then is it not reasonable to believe that the breath of God is spirit. In addition to that, when He created us, we were created in purity. Our spirit or soul, started out pure. In fact, everything associated with God that He created was pure. In Genesis, He called it good. The one item that God gave Adam and Eve that changed the balance was their freewill. With it, they corrupted the purity of the spirit or soul that God had given them. As we enter further in the discussion, we will discuss freewill more. However, I inserted this section on the soul's immortality to forewarn those who may have a different view, the soul's immortality is a view taken for granted in this book.

Chapter II

BEFORE THE WORLD WAS CREATED

We will start by looking at what the Bible says about before the world was created. We will do so by examining what we can decipher from what Paul wrote in Ephesians. Later we will also look at what John said about Jesus in the beginning. We will examine Paul's statement by looking at it from a different interpretation than traditionally interpreted. However, we are not trying to change the traditional interpretation, but perhaps decipher a deeper meaning from it. We will look at it as it is literally written. From our examination we will pull out some crucial points that others may have failed to examine or bring out in the main theme Christian theology. We will examine the possibility of souls existing with God before He created the world. From this examination, we will see what we can decipher from scripture about what the criterion is or would be for souls to live with God eternally. By understanding this criterion, it will lay the foundation for further discussion to help us to move forward with added clarity.

I believe that God has given us clues throughout His word about Himself and allows us to discover them through the leading of His

Holy spirit. As mentioned earlier, I don't understand why I even began to write this book or even the one prior that I referenced. Although I do know why, I pray that God guides me and provides me with insight into His word as I try to share what I believe He has placed within me to share. While writing, I constantly ask him to remove my own selfish desires to expound on what I think I am capable of reasoning and replace them with the words of His will and not mine. As I write the following, I pray that it is insight from Him and not of my own misguided logic. I explain this because some of the following statements do not follow traditional teaching of these verses.

The Criterion to Live with God

"What is the criterion to live with God in eternity and what are the requirements?" Does this criterion of living with God have an effect on souls here on earth? To answer what the requirements are to live with God, we will examine Ephesians 1, verses 35. In these verses we can find several points indicating the requirements. The first criterion to live with God from these verses is that we must be in Him to be holy. The second criterion is we must be blameless of sin before Him. This is the way the (NKJV New King James Version) and the (NLT New Living Translation) state it in Ephesian1:35 below.

Ephesians 1:3-5 (NKJV))
3 Blessed be the God and Father of our Lord Jesus Christ, who has blessed us with every spiritual blessing in the heavenly places in Christ, 4 just as He chose us in Him before the foundation of the world, that we should be holy and without blame before Him in love, 5 having predestined us to adoption as sons by Jesus Christ to Himself, according to the good pleasure of His will.

Ephesians 1:3-5 (NLT)
3 All praise to God, the Father of our Lord Jesus Christ, who has blessed us with every spiritual blessing in the heavenly realms because we are united with Christ. 4 Even before he made the

world, God loved us and chose us in Christ to be holy and without fault in his eyes. 5 God decided in advance to adopt us into his own family by bringing us to himself through Jesus Christ. This is what he wanted to do, and it gave him great pleasure.

From the verses above, we can see that the criterion to live with God is to be holy and without fault in God's eyes. In addition, when we break these verses down and look at them literally as they are written; something else stands out in them.

They tell us something about the state of souls living with God. Note that the preceding statement said souls living with God. I stated it in that manner because I believe that the verses we just read in Ephesians give an indication to that fact as the beginning verses in Jerimiah. To this end, I believe souls live preexisting lives with God prior to inhabiting mortal flesh. To get a more in depth discussion of why I believe it, read my previous book, Why are we here and from where did we come, Answered.

However, the point that is being made here is, when souls live with God, they are pure from sin and faultless in God's eyes. Verse four supports both the preexisting view and the holy and faultless point of view if we take the statement literally as it was written. "Even before he made the world, God loved us and chose us in Christ to be holy and without fault in his eyes."

Taking the first part of the verse literally, we see that God loved us (our souls) even before He made the world. What support the fact that the verse could be referencing our souls and not our mortal bodies? There are two things that I believe support this thought. The first point is obvious because the verse says before He made the world He loved us. Our mortal bodies were not there. The second point that supports the idea, is that the whole story of the Bible is about the love that God has for our souls. He gave His only begotten Son to die for the salvation of our souls or to put it another way, for our souls to return to Him.

Therefore, by accepting the view that souls preexist with God, we can reason that when a soul comes into the body, it is without sin. It is pure and innocent. Even if one rejects the preexisting view and accepts the creationist view of souls, which is that God creates a new soul for each newborn, the same fact that souls are pure from sin when entering into the body is supported from reading Genesis. Everything God created or creates is good and not sinful. However, I take the preexisting souls' view because the complete concept, as put forth in my previous book, supports and deepens the concept of God's unselfish love.

As we continue to examine the verses in Ephesians we get more enlighten about the relationship God had with us prior to creation. I believe that the message that God gave Paul may have had more depth than Paul understood at the time because the second possible meaning wasn't the message that God wanted delivered because it did not meet the needs of the people at the time. Let's look at these verses more intently and see what they say that God did prior to creation.

I believe Paul states two important ideas in Ephesians 1:4 that set up the rest of the verse. They were alluded to above. The first is *"before God made the world"*. The second is *"God loved us"*. Of the two points, the second one is the one that we pick up on as being most important to us because it is. However, because God's love is the most important thing to us, I believe we miss the point of when the love began and in doing so miss a possible underlining meaning in the message?

After Paul states these two points, he states the actions God took prior to Him making the world. *He chose us in Christ to be Holy and blameless in His sight.* We generally agree that God did the choosing before He created the world, but it is generally taken to imply a future action that Christ would take and took here on earth after Christ came. However, I believe that God's action can be viewed in a different way also. Let's look at *"He chose us in Christ to be Holy and blameless in His sight"* and examine it. This makes a statement that we may pass over without giving it the thought it might deserve. God chose us in Christ before He made the world could mean exactly what it says and that Christ was there with Him and we (our souls) were created through Christ at that time. We ignore the part of the statement that "this happened before He made the world" could also imply that God did exactly what the statement says He did, before He made the world. In addition, this view also helps us understand the verse in Jeremiah where God told him He knew him before he was in his mother's womb. It also helps us understand John 1:14 and also goes along with it. "In the beginning the Word already existed. The Word was with God, and the Word was God. He existed in the beginning with God. God created everything through him, and nothing was created except through him. The Word gave life to everything that was created, and his life brought light to everyone. When we look at these verses together, I believe they make a compelling argument for the point of view I am taking.

Nevertheless, actions in Ephesians have been traditionally projected to refer totally to actions Christ took here on the earth after He made the world. As we continue reading, the next verse, *"God decided in advance to adopt us into his own family by bringing us to himself through Jesus Christ,"* to me, clearly explains what God decided in advance that He would do in the future for mankind here on earth through Christ. Adopting us into His family was and is an act that verses 6 and 7 explain that Christ did on the cross which took place after the creation. For those of us who choose to be in Christ again, are restored back through Christ to holiness and blamelessness in God's sight. When we break down or parse the verse even more we ask, "What is meant by 'in God's sight'?"

I believe this means that God is the judge of our holiness and blamelessness. Although we here have fallen into sin and become unholy, God accepts our holiness and blamelessness through the righteous blood of His Son, Jesus. John pointed out, that we were created in the beginning and made righteous through Him. Now our souls are once again made holy and blamelessness through His shed blood. Once this occurs, God elevates us because we have learned the lesson of how much He loves us by accepting the fact that He loved us enough to give up His son so our undeserving souls could return to Him. Christ's death performed the act of adopting us into His holy family and giving us a more intimate relationship with God. We demonstrated our understanding of God's love for us and what love really is by confessing our belief in Christ the - example of His love.

Let's look at the adoption process and the meaning of a more intimate relationship to explain them clearer. To do so, we must again return to the preexisting concept of the soul and look at the relationship between God and souls prior to creation. We know what type of relationship God had with souls because Paul tells us He loved them, but we do not know what type of relationship souls had with God. However, we can discern the type of relationship from reading the Scriptures with spiritually un-blinded minds. When we get to Adam and Eve in Genesis, we will see that Adam and Eve had no knowledge of good and evil. We will discover other things about Adam and Eve which will reflect back to their souls' newness to a difference existence. However, since we are talking about existence before the creation of the world, let's continue talking about souls and see if we can lay some foundations for souls' unawareness of good and evil. We will begin by looking at what I believe was and is our souls' journey.

The Soul's Journey

When we get to Adam and Eve, we will also learn that they did not have emotions because they did not become afraid or ashamed until they ate from *the tree of the knowledge of good and evil*. Because these things will be mentioned in the story, I believe they have significance. I believe they help shed a light on the state of souls with God prior to their earthly journey.

If souls preexist with God as I believe is supported in scripture, the state of souls prior to earth's journey was and is void of the ability to know what love really means. Our souls' journey here equips our souls with the ability to experience love and understand the true love that God has for us and had prior to our journey. As Paul stated in Ephesians 1:4, *"Even before he made the world, God loved us..."* I also have come to consider that He loved us so much, that is the reason we are here. Since God is eternal and God created souls immortal in His eternal realm, they would have always been with Him. Perhaps, God wanted to give them an opportunity to choose their own destiny. So out of love for them, He wanted them to be able to choose their own destiny and at the same time understand the depth of His love for them. Once they did understand, first what love was and secondly how much He loved them, they could receive a promotion in a sense; into the intimate family of God. However, it required them to understand what love really was to be able to appreciate being in His intimate family. Knowing that they had nothing to compare love with, He planned a way for them to do so. He created a nonimmortal existence for them to experience. He created mankind and provided souls the ability to have freewill to choose their destiny. By doing so, our souls would come to know what His love is by accepting the fact that He loved us enough to sacrifice His son for us even after we failed and continue to fail the initial test. The Gospel of John drives this point home. *"For God so loved the world: He gave his one and only Son, so that everyone who believes in him will not perish but have eternal life.* This acceptance through belief allows God to give our souls a promotion through Christ's adoption of us into His Holy family. Even though our souls were initially there with God in His presence from the time He created us, we still were not intimately a part of His holy family. We did not know or understand the true love God had for us. We could not understand His true love for us because we had nothing to contrast it against. Therefore, we did not have the full knowledge of what love really meant, and we could not return intimate love to God. In addition, we did not have the opportunity to choose where to spend eternity. God loved us unselfishly enough to give us that opportunity.

He gave and gives us that opportunity to make the first step to accept eternity with Him and to become His adopted children. We do this by coming to an initial acceptance of God's love for us by simply believing that Jesus Christ is His son and the acceptance of His salvation through His sacrificial death on the cross and His resurrection. This process of adoption brings us into a more intimate relationship with Him than we could have had without it. It allows us to show reciprocal love for God's agape love toward us. That is, we learn a more intimate love for God because we can now recognize how much He loves us and now know what love is and how to love. In other words, if we had always stayed in paradise, we would not have been able to understand what it would be like being out of paradise.

We can see from Paul's letter to the Ephesians why God took the actions He did prior and after creation. He took them because He loved us prior to the creation and He continued to love us even after we fell and fall by sin here on earth. To insure that we could be holy and blameless in His sight after the creation and our fall, as we were before the creation, He planned and made a way for that to occur. He made a cleanup plan beforehand which shows that He knew our pure innocent souls would become corrupted. So, If God knew our souls would become corrupted, why did He not make us so they would not? This question has been asked over the ages but I believe I have provided a plausible answer. I believe it is because of God's love for our souls and His desire to give us the freedom to choose to be with him eternally and to give us the ability to experience love so we could have a more intimate relationship with Him. He demonstrated to us the type and depth of love He desires for us by initially giving us up to allow us the freedom to choose to leave Him eternally or return to Him eternally. Secondly and most importantly, He gave up His son, out of love for our souls, to die for us. Our souls died but through Christ, we are restored to eternal life to return to Him more Glorified than when we left. He did this because He knew that only through us understanding how much He loved us we could accept and try to emulate His unconditional love which qualifies us for adoption into His family. Understanding this type of love allows us to have that close intimate family love with Him and other souls. God continues to demonstrate it for us through Christ continuing forgiveness, mercy and grace. The most important thing is that He made it easy for us to become members of His family by simply believing who Christ is and choosing that love through the acceptance of Christ as His son.

Summary of Criterion to Live with God

We have used these verses in Ephesians to reinforce several points in our earlier discussion. From these verses coupled with Jeremiah, we can see that before God made the world, He knew and loved our souls. Therefore, we believe our souls existed with Him prior to their earthly journey. We also see that for souls to exist with God, they must be holy and blameless. Therefore, souls that exist with God prior to their earthly journey live in a sinless place because they are already with God absent from sin. Because of this pure existence, when souls enter into a mortal host, us, they enter pure, holy and blameless to begin an experience that they never had before. The fact that souls enter our bodies pure and holy to begin their new experience is a crucial point to remember. This new experience is for the ability to have and exercise freewill and to experience all the benefits and nonbenefits that come with it. However we know some of the earthly benefits. Romans 8:28 states for those who love God." ... God causes everything to work together for the good of those who love God and are called according to his purpose for them. We also know the heavenly benefit; we can be adopted into the family of God for a fuller and a more abundant life with Him in eternity. The gift of freewill is solely for the purpose to choose or not to choose to return to live eternally with God as part of his family. When we do not choose to do so, it is because we fail to recognize the love God has for us and in turn fail to love Him back.

Ironically, we as Christians already know that our souls were once with God. We voice it often without thought of what we are really saying. Many times, Christians talk about going home to live with God. If we are going home, then we are saying that we are going back to a place where we have already come. Home is a familiar place, not a strange place. We are really saying that our eternal souls are going home since we will shed this mortal body and take on our eternal one. 1 Corinthians 15:53 states it like this, "For our dying bodies must be transformed into bodies that will never die; our mortal bodies must be transformed into immortal bodies."

When we sum it all up, the criterion to live with God is simply to accept that He loved us enough to develop a plan of creation and redemption and made sacrifices so we can experience what His love is like. He decided all of this before He created the world and did it all out of love for our souls.

Chapter III

AFTER CREATION

As we continue to explore different aspects of the Bible, I hope that each reader will come to the conclusion that God is still executing His plan of salvation that He made before the creation of the world to provide souls the opportunity to make the choice between a more abundant eternal life with Him or an eternal existence away from him. In addition to Him executing his plan, He has given us markers in the Bible to follow so we can be sure that He is God and the Bible is His divine guided word. As we look at the stories of the beginning of mankind and the birth of the nation of Israel and God's deliverance of His chosen children, we will hear God specifically saying that there are things He is doing so that people will know He is God. When we finally arrive at the cross and examine Christ's statement, we will more clearly see its far reaching meaning. Let's begin our journey through part of the Bible by looking at some of the familiar Bible stories from the Old Testament and see if we can decipher what they are teaching.

Earlier we discussed the soul prior to the world's creation. Now we will begin to look at the souls actions after creation. To do this, we must begin looking at the beginning of mankind. For a biblical perspective we must start at the story of Adam and Eve. As Christians, we believe that all of mankind's trouble and as we hope to find, mankind's final joy began with them. In the story, God creates them in a spiritually immortal state and gives them an abundant amount of choices of trees to choose fruit from which to eat. Then He gives them one tree from which they cannot eat. So, Adam and Eve are placed in a precarious situation. They must make a monumental decision. They can eat from a large number of different trees or choose to eat from this one forbidden tree. They really had a hard decision before them; eat from the big bowl of goodies that God had given them, or eat out of the bowl that contained only one thing. What seemed the most logical thing to do? We will look at what they did and discuss some surprising things about their actions.

Adam & Eve

Obviously, they choose to eat from the bowl that contained the one object. It was the bowl that God had told them not to dip their hands into. God knew that once they did, it would break the perfect spiritual bond they had with Him and that they would find themselves naked, uncovered and spiritually dead.

We see from Scripture that is exactly what happened. They immediately lost their covering and they realized that they were naked. However, the fact that they were naked shouldn't have been a big surprise for them, because they had always been naked; so nothing had changed in the physical sense. Yet they sensed they were naked. They knew that they needed cover, so they sought it. Even though they had covered themselves, they knew that the covering had not solved the problem. Something else was wrong with them. They still felt they were naked. We will discuss the why later. What they did not realize, was that they were dead. However, in addition to feeling naked, they were feeling something that they had never experienced before. It was fear. They heard God and they hid. When God quizzed them, they had to come clean. But there is some subtlety in the conversation with God that we sometime miss. Let's look at the conversation.

Genesis 3:9-11: *"But the Lord God called to the man, "Where are you?" He answered, "I heard you in the garden, and I was afraid because I was naked; so I hid." And he said, "Who told you that you were naked? Have you eaten from the tree that I commanded you not to eat from?"*

We read in Genesis 3:67 that they sewed fig leaves and made an apron. Genesis 3:67 *"And when the woman saw that the tree was good for food, and that it was pleasant to the eyes, and a tree to be desired to make one wise, she took of the fruit thereof, and did eat, and gave also unto her husband with her; and he did eat. And the eyes of them both were opened, and they knew that they were naked; and they sewed fig leaves together, and made themselves aprons."*

Prior to God's coming Adam and Eve had already clothed themselves with fig leaves. Yet, from his answer to God, we know that Adam still felt his nakedness although he had been partially covered with fig leaves. So technically they were no longer naked. So, why did Adam still feel naked although he was obviously partially clothed from the fig leaves? It is because that is exactly what he was? He had become uncovered from the loss of God's Holy Spirit. At times, we can relate to Adams feelings of nakedness. When we sin and go contrary to God's will, we feel a sense of nakedness; that is, somewhat away from God. Yet, just as Adam was, before we became Christians, we were naked but still partially clothed; covered from God's plan of salvation that He had made before He created the world. We will later discuss the statement God made to Adam that let us know that God had not forgotten His master plan. In fact, Adam's and Eve's sins pull the master plan into action.

There is another very important part of this story that we have not talked about. Can you think of what it is? Let's go back to Genesis and see what we left out that is so important. Now as we read the following verses from Genesis 2:1718 and Genesis 3:45, which took place before Adam's and Eve's sins, watch the sequence of events as they occurred.

Genesis 2:1718 "You are free to eat from any tree in the garden; but you must not eat from the tree of the knowledge of good and evil, for when you eat from it you will certainly die." The Lord God said, "It is not good for the man to be alone. I will make a helper suitable for him."

We see in Chapter 2, God told Adam that He was free to eat from any tree in the garden except one. We also see that God told him there would be consequence if he did. The consequence God told him was death. However, let's think more about what God told him not to do that would bring the consequence of death. This is a very important piece of information we are about to zero in on. God told him not to eat from *the tree of the knowledge of good and evil.* After you think about that, answer the following question. *Did Adam know that he was doing evil or wrong when he ate from the tree?* The answer to this question leads us into deeper discussion and launches us onward to the cross. In addition, the consequence of their actions is also important in our discussion. The consequence was death. In fact, God made it completely clear by saying, "You will certainly die." However, the sequence of events that I want noticed is what God said after warning Adam about not eating from the tree that would bring death. God then said it was not good for Adam to be alone, so He would make a helper **suitable** for him.

The thing to notice is that God just had forbidden Adam to eat from the forbidden tree and announced death on him if he did, then immediately afterwards, God created the **suitable helper** who led Adam to do what God had explicitly told him not to do. I find that strange, but it also says to me that everything that happened was part of God's plan that He had made before He made the world. Here we can begin to see hints about God overall plan to allow souls the freedom to choose to spend eternity with Him as adopted children or spend eternity away from Him. The phrase, *"souls the freedom to choose"*, is mentioned here because a further discussion of this will occur later. In addition, I just indicated that it was in God's plan that Eve would be tempted by the serpent which is representative of Satan. If that is the case, why would God develop a plan that allowed mankind the ability to be outside of His will? We will also look at what I believe is a possible answer to this question further into our discussion.

However, even before we move on, let's look at the start of the ongoing battle started with Adam's and Eve's act of disobedience. Genesis 3:15 God placed a curse on the serpent and made this statement to it. *"And I will put enmity between you and the woman, and between your offspring and hers; he will crush your head, and you will strike his heel."* This was the first sign of Jesus coming and His removal of the action that Satan's temptation on Eve brought about. It is important to remember what the action of their sin brought about. In addition, to this early indication of Christ's coming, there is found in Genesis even more detailed evidence of Christ coming and God's plan of salvation.

In the fifth chapter of Genesis, the lineage of Adam down to Noah is given. Is this just a historical record of Adam's linage or is there more to it? The answer is no. It is not just a historical linage record, and yes there is more to it. There is a very important message given here. When the meaning of Adam and his descendants' names are displayed, it shows that the meaning of their Hebrew names in the lineage tree writes out the following message.

Adam means **Man**, Seth means **appointed**, Enosh means **mortal**, Kenan means **sorrow**, Mahalalel means **the blessed God**, Jared means **shall come down**, Enoch means **teaching**, Methuselah means **his**

death shall bring, Lamech means **the despairing**, and Noah means **comfort or rest**. When these meaning are put together the message is **"Man appointed mortal sorrow, the blessed God shall come down teaching his death shall bring the despairing comfort or rest."**

One of the purposes of this discussion and others is to show that God created a plan for our souls to develop a closer relationship with Him and He wants us to know that plan. He has given markers along the way in His word to help us discover His plan. However, He wants us to search His word in order that we will come to know Him and His ways more clearly. We will see as we progress, God's teaching started with Adam and Eve at the creation and continues on today. As we continue to look at some of the common stories of the Bible, I believe we will discover other hidden messages and indications of future events that we may have overlooked in past readings. However, before we leave Adam and Eve, we will go into further discussion about the consequences of their actions and take a look at perhaps why they did what they did. To do this, we must consider the root cause **inherent in them** for their action. We often blame our actions on the sin that many say that was inherited from Adam and Eve. If that is the case, then we must ask the question, why did Adam and Eve sin? They did not inherit sin from anyone. I believe we sin for the same reason they did. However, their sin did bring on the consequence of sin for everyone. Remember what God told Adam and Eve the consequence was for their sin of disobedience. To try to get an understanding of why Adam and Eve took the actions they did, we will consider freewill and its relationship to sin.

Freewill and its Problem - Sin

We mentioned earlier, in summarizing the criterion to live with God, freewill's benefits and non-benefits. But what is freewill? Is it just the ability to choose? The answer is no. Freewill is more than just the ability to choose and make a choice as we will see later. However, coming into a new type of existence with this new ability of freewill brought about problems for Adam and Eve and brings about problems for us. As we continue to examine the creation story of Adam and Eve, we will get a clearer picture of how this presented a problem to them. In the young adult Church School class that I teach, I often go back to the story of Adam and Eve. I believe the story of the creation as told in Genesis through the creation story lays a foundational basis for the salvation story, and the development of mankind into a spiritual being; a being whose understanding of the creator continually grows to a higher understanding of God's love for our souls. We will use the creation story to start the examination of this growth and move upward to the culminating event marking the depth of God's love by Christ's ultimate sacrifice and His statement signifying God's purpose for His reason of coming. We have already looked at some of the foundational verses in the creation story that we will be discussing, and we will refer back to specific verses in our discussions in hope to obtain deeper understanding from them.

By continuing to look at man's initial fall, we will examine the beginning of man's understanding of who God is, and we will also see what I believe was Satan's rise to power. It may also be looked at, in a sense, the beginning of his defeat and also his gain of power. In our upcoming discussions we will examine more closely *what is sin, the birth of sin, Satan's beginning and the beginning of Satan's defeat, what Satan's start of defeat mean, the power gain of Satan, and the role of mankind's freewill in sin's occurrence.*

What is sin?

Freewill is the ability to have and exercise a will different from God's will. In other words, it is the ability for the soul to be disobedient to God. Adam and Eve were the first beings recorded in Scripture with souls able to do this. Therefore, sin is being outside of God's will through the act of disobedience from the use of mankind's freedom to be outside of God's will. When we look and define sin as such, we see that Satan's corruption of his wisdom does not fit that criterion of sin. Therefore the act of tempting Adam and Eve was not outside of God's will as defined by sin. God did not forbid him not to tempt Adam and Eve. Now I am not saying that Satan acts in accordance to God's will. So, this brings about another question which we will discuss in fuller detail later. *Does Satan have free will, and if so, is Satan's will which is outside of God's will, categorized as sin?*

The Birth of Sin

Some consider Satan's act of tempting Eve was the first sin and call it *Satan's sin of pride.* Based, on our previous discussion and the definition of sin as being disobedient to God, Satan's act can't be categorized as sin. If the belief that the first sin was *"Satan's sin of pride"* is not valid, then what was the first sin? Let's look at the Scriptures more closely to see if we can answer this question from a spiritually logical view. Although, some Theologians say that the first sin was the sin of pride committed by Satan in the Garden, does Scripture validate that? I don't think it does. So, let's see why. Here is one Scripture that I believe disputes the claim outright. Roman 5:12 (KJV): *Wherefore, as by one man sin entered into the world, and death by sin; and so death passed upon all men, for that all have sinned.* As we can see from this Scripture, Paul clearly states that Adam brought sin into the world; not Satan but let's not just stop here. I believe the key words here are "Sin into the world." We will see why a little later.

Since the serpent in the Garden of Eden is said to be Satan, he was there. But what does Scripture say about him in the garden? Scripture says in Genesis 3:1 (NKJV), *"Now the serpent was more cunning than any beast of the field which the Lord God had made."* When we read it closely, we see that Scripture does not say here that the serpent or Satan was evil or sinful. It says cunning or smarter. We will discuss the question of Satan being evil later.

Since sin is the act of disobedience to God, there is no account in Genesis of Satan act of disobedience to God. There is the account of Adam's and Eve's disobedience. Therefore, sin was brought into existence by Adam's and Eve's disobedience against God. Prior to Adam's and Eve's disobedience there was no sin because it was the first opportunity Satan had to persuade souls to be disobedient to God. So, was Satan's act of persuasion an act of sin?

Since the serpent in the garden is representative of Satan, he was responsible for the enticement of mankind's first act of sin which was the act of disobedience to God. However, note that Scripture doesn't say the serpent was disobedient to God. It says it was more cunning. It was cursed because it enticed Adam and Eve to be disobedient; not because he sinned or was disobedient to God. The same remains true today, Satan doesn't commit the sin charged against us; he entices us to do so. So Adam's and Eve's disobedience was the birth of sin.

If Adam and Eve's sin was the birth of sin and Satan does not sin, what was John 3:8 saying about Satan and sin? *1John 3:8 "The one practicing sin is of the devil, because the devil sins from the beginning. For this the Son of God was revealed, that He might undo the works of the devil."*

I believe the meaning of this verse is not to imply that Satan committed the first sin, but sin came about in the beginning because of Satan's influence and we have been enticed by it throughout. The second part of the verse explains what Christ did for us to nullify the works of the devil. Christ did not undo the sin of the devil; He undid the result of the act of sin done by man from the enticement of the devil. Man is forgiven through Christ. Satan is not. Christ forgiveness of the sin of the world was and is universal to mankind. When we read John 1:29, we see the purpose of Christ coming... *"Behold! The Lamb of God who takes away the sin of the world!"* Note, that He came to take away the SIN of the world, not the **SINS** of the world. Satan did not commit the SIN of the world. He caused the SIN of the world and sin in the world to be committed. Since man did bring sin into the world, would man have sin if he did not have freewill?

The Role of Mankind's Freewill in Sin's Occurrence

God opened the door of opportunity to Satan so that he would have an avenue in which to tempt Eve. What was the open door of opportunity? Was it freewill? If it was freewill, would sin exist without it?" In earlier discussions, we said that sin came from Adam's and Eves' ability to exercise their will to be disobedient; placing their will in opposition to God's will. We defined that as freewill. Adam's and Eve's sins originated from direct disobedience of God's command. God specifically told them not to do a specific thing. The thing that God told them not to do was something that made them aware of their wrong doing. Therefore, they were not aware that what they were doing was evil and what it really meant to do it.

We talk a lot about freewill, but what is freewill? Is it the ability to make choices or is it more than just making choices? What choices did Adam and Eve have in the garden and were all the choices freewill choices? Remember that God told them that they could eat from all the other trees in the garden but could not eat from *the tree of the knowledge of good and evil.* Therefore, they had many choices of different fruits from which to choose. So, how many freewill choices did they have? The answer is one. So what was it? Was it to eat or not to eat from the forbidden tree? Perhaps surprisingly, the answer is no. It was to remain within the will of God. By acting outside of the will of God, their souls exercised their freewill for the first time. Prior to this, their souls had always been in God's will. This act of disobedience to God's will was, as we said earlier, the first sin. The first recorded prohibition that God made to any created entity was not to eat from the forbidden tree.

Also, as we stated earlier, God had not forbidden Satan to tempt Eve. As shown from the Scripture account of Job, Satan is subservient to God especially when dealing with God's people. Satan would not have had the opportunity to do so if God had not provided Adam's and Eve's souls the ability to be outside of His will by providing them freewill. In order for them to have freewill, there had to be a choice lying outside of His will and something to draw them to it. Satan was the something that provided the draw or the temptation. As soon as they yielded to his will instead of God's will by using their freewill ability, they knew for the <u>first time</u> the difference between good and evil. They knew that something had changed in their relationship with God and they demonstrated it through their actions. That one act of freewill by the soul made freewill the birthing mechanism for sin.

The Beginning of Satan's Defeat and Power Gain

The serpent in the Garden of Eden is depicted as representing Satan. If the serpent is representative of Satan, there is reason to believe that the beginning of his defeat and rise to power occurred at the same time of man's initial fall. Many believe that other Scriptures describe Satan's fall as being kicked out of Heaven and thrown to the earth, and they hold to the view Satan's pride was the first sin and also the cause of his fall. Although we discussed this briefly above, let's look at it again through the creation story and other Scriptures to find if there is valid support for the claim of Satan's pride being the first sin.

Two Scriptures some subscribe to as accounts of Satan's fall from grace and to the earth are Ezekiel 28 and Isaiah 14:1215. They may or may not be. If they are, at least one seems to place Satan's fall at the time of Adam's and Eve's. Others use Revelation to refer to the fall of Satan. However, I believe the description given in Revelation refers to a future defeat of Satan. However, some reject that.

Those who do not believe that Ezekiel and Isaiah are intended as a description of Satan's fall believe they are clearly references referring to kings. Ezekiel is referring to the King of Tyre and Isaiah is referring to the King of Babylon. I tend to agree with those who take this view. However, I will use the Ezekiel Scripture to show how it can be used to support that his fall occurred in the Garden of Eden. As I alluded to earlier, I believe Satan's fall was in the Garden simultaneously with mankind's fall and also had a power gain at the same time. I will take snippets from Ezekiel to support the assertion that the fall of Satan was in the Garden of Eden at the same time Adam and Eve's fall took place.

Part of Ezekiel 28:12-13 read, "…*You were the seal of perfection, full of wisdom and perfect in beauty. You were in Eden, the garden of God…*" Ezekiel 28:17 says, "*Your heart was lifted up because of your beauty; You corrupted your wisdom for the sake of your splendor; I cast you to the ground…*"

Part of this statement, "You were the seal of perfection, full of wisdom", can be used to support the fact as stated in Genesis that the Serpent was more cunning than other creatures. He showed that he had more knowledge about God than Adam and Eve, and used his cunning ability and knowledge to entice Eve's disobedience, thus corrupting his wisdom. Another part of it, "I cast you to the ground", can be used to imply God's curse on the Serpent to crawl on its belly as a representation of his fall from grace.

Although I used snippets from Ezekiel to support the assertion that Satan's so call fall was in the garden, I believe the validity of the assertion that it is a depiction of Satan's fall, is not true in the sense those who assert it believe. However, if one view the fall of Satan as his curse, the fall of Satan at the time of mankind's fall, does fit scripturally logical in the story of the fall in the Garden; but what does it really imply? Let's examine the logic of it. If Satan's job is to allow mankind's soul a choice to choose God's will or be outside of His will, the first place and time God provided souls this opportunity was in the garden at mankind's creation. However, I don't believe that the garden was the first place Satan corrupted his wisdom and I don't believe his act was considered sin. So, if Satan's corruption of his wisdom was not sin or the first sin, what was it?

Earlier when we talked about whether the first sin came into the world from Adam and Eve or from Satan, another question about Satan and freewill arose. The question was, "Was Satan given freewill and if so, is Satan's will outside of God's will categorized as sin?"

Many deduce from Scriptures such as Job, which reference Satan in relationship to angels that Satan was a fallen angel and further deduce that Satan, as other angels, has freewill. If we accept that deduction, then it is logical to conclude that Satan's will is in opposition to God's will and conclude that Satan did commit the first sin. However, this conclusion may not be as valid as it may seem. After considering other factors, we must also ask, *"Does Satan's will, being in opposition to God's will, qualify as sin the same as mankind's, and did his opposition come before the creation of the world?"* We have based most of our discussion on the belief in the preexisting theory of souls. This concept assumes that souls existed prior to the creation of Adam's and Eve's world. If souls existed, then other heavenly host existed. Nehemiah makes reference to God creating the heavens and the heaven of heavens where heavenly host preside. (Nehemiah 9:6) *"You alone are the Lord; You have made heaven, the heaven of heavens, with all their host, the earth and everything on it, the seas and all that is in them, and You preserve them all. The host of heaven worships You."* Considering this point, perhaps Satan could have committed the first offence of portraying a will in opposition to God's prior to the creation of the earth in the *"heavens of heavens"*. Even if he did or did not, we must consider whether we can call Satan's opposition to God, sin in the same context as we do Adam's and Eve's sins. In considering this, we must look at what sin is, what sin did and the fact that God had prepared a cure for it. Then we must ask if Satan's actions can be placed into the same category. If they cannot, then we can't consider them as the same type of sin as mankind's sin.

Adam's and Eve's sins originated from direct disobedience of God's command and being tempted by the serpent. God specifically told them not to do a specific thing. As we mentioned earlier, the thing that God told them not to do was something that made them aware that their act of disobedience was evil. Therefore, they were not aware of the fact that what they were doing was evil in God's sight and what it really meant. However, from the text in Genesis, we see that Satan was already aware of what the forbidden fruit would produce. The text also tells us why. He was craftier than the other animals which included Adam and Eve. We can conclude that craftier also meant smarter, since the text told us that Satan knew that once they ate from the fruit, their eyes would be opened and they would know good from evil. This is important because it leads to the question of why Satan could have been smarter. Turning to Scripture again, we might be able to get some indication. We hear David saying in Psalm 8:4-5, *"What is mankind that you are mindful of them, human beings that you care for them? You have made them a little lower than the angels and crowned them with glory and honor..."* and also the writer of Hebrews 2:6-7 echoes the same. Since Satan is as many Theologians believe, a fallen angel, then he was created higher than mankind and had a higher level of understanding of what it meant to be in opposition of God's will. Because of this, his decision to be outside of God's will was and is different than mankind's decision. He had no tempting power to lead him in opposition to God's will; it was his own desire to be in opposition to God. His reason was and is to overthrow God's kingdom. He knew the totality of the consequences of his actions before he made them because he already knew the difference between good and evil. He knew that being in opposition to God's will, would separate him from God. Earlier we said that we would discuss Satan's evilness.

Since God was and is all good, then Satan's willful choice to separate himself from God, made him evil. In fact, since up until that time only good existed, Satan's separation made him the initial entity of evil and thus encompassed all evil representing total opposition to God's holy will. The tree of the knowledge of good and evil existed only because of Satan initial opposition of God. Man on the other hand did not know and doesn't know the full consequences of his sinful acts and desires that come from deception by Satan. It may be argued that Satan's rebellion against God had to have occurred prior to the incident in the garden in order for him to have already been in opposition to God's will to tempt Adam and Eve to be outside of God's will. On the other hand, if his desire came about from the fact that it was the first time he had an opportunity to persuade mankind outside of God's will, his actions still do not qualify as sin in the same manner as Adam's and Eve's did or mankind's does.

If it did, then Satan would be included in God's plan of redemption. However, his knowing and willful choice of rebellion doomed him eternally and set up the struggle we all now have trying to be obedient to God. Therefore, the answers to questions of Satan's freewill and Satan's original sin, is yes to freewill, but no to Satan committing the first sin. His rebellion was and is different from mankind's sin of disobedience from Satan's temptation. It is a more serious offence directed at God's supremacy. His actions are not forgivable and therefore are in another class other than sin.

What Satan's Start of Defeat Means

We have implied that Satan's start of defeat occurred in the garden at the time of Adam's and Eve's fall. Let's examine the reasoning behind this statement and exactly what is meant by it. If Satan's actions in the garden were not counted as sin, why was he cursed? Since his curse occurred after Adam's and Eve's sins, his curse came because of their sin. Therefore, Satan's start of defeat, as meant here - as his curse, came at the time of the first act of sin by Adam and Eve. Although some make the claim that the first sin was Satan's sin of pride, but as we have shown that claim doesn't stand up under close scrutiny. Let's look at the sequence of occurrences in the garden to get further clarification. Adam and Eve sinned. Their sin was a result of Satan's enticement. However, up to the point that they became disobedient, sin still had not occurred. No disobedience had taken place. Because of his enticement, Eve's will, became in opposition to God's will.

> Genesis 3:13-14 (NKJV) States: *And the Lord God said to the woman, "What is this you have done?" The woman said, "The serpent deceived me, and I ate." So the Lord God said to the serpent: "Because you have done this, You are cursed more than all cattle, And more than every beast of the field; On your belly you shall go, And you shall eat dust." And I will put enmity Between you and the woman, And between your seed and her Seed; He shall bruise your head, And you shall bruise His heel."*

Note that the results of Satan's enticement did not occur until Eve acted on them. If Eve would not have acted, and his attempt had not been fruitful, would he have received the curse? He was not cursed until after the act took place by Eve and Adam. His curse came about because of what he did. He caused Adam and Eve to sin by his enticement. So the start of his defeat occurred because Eve succumbed to his enticement. The start of his defeat was the curse; *"And I will put enmity Between you and the woman, And between your seed and her Seed;* **He** *shall bruise your head, And you shall bruise* **His heel**.*"* It was God promise that Christ would bring defeat to him. However, his successful act of deception and temptation was also a gain of power for him.

The Power Gain of Satan from Mankind's fall

We stated earlier that God opened the door of opportunity to Satan so that Satan would have an avenue in which to tempt Eve. This was done before Eve acted on Satan's attempt. It was the first time that God allowed him the possibility to detract souls from God's will. How do I know that God allowed him? First, God made him smart enough to know what *the tree of the knowledge of good and evil* was and did. He knew once Adam and Eve ate from it they would know the difference between good and evil. He knew once they did, that it would provide him a better path way to them. They would lose the covering of God's Holy Spirit. God's hedge or fence would be removed from around them.

Secondly, it is made clear that Satan has to have God's permission to perform his acts on those of God. Job 1:8, 11-12 states: *Then the Lord said to Satan, "Have you considered My servant Job, that there is **none like him on the earth**, a **blameless and upright** man, one who fears God and shuns evil?" But now, stretch out Your hand and touch all that he has, and he will surely curse You to Your face!" And the Lord said to Satan, "Behold, all that he has is in your power; only do not lay a hand on his person."* So from the example of Job, we see that Satan has to have God's permission to come after those of God; and at the time, both Adam and Eve, were God's totally. Their souls had not been corrupted. They were **blameless and upright. None like them was on the earth**. Just as a side bar, note how the description about Job fits Adam and Eve. They still had God's covering; they were not yet naked of God's Holy Spirit. However, He had removed His hedge from around them as he did later with Job. He removed His hedge by giving them freewill.

However, I should note two differences between Job and Adam and Eve. Job feared God and knew to shun evil. Adam and Eve had not yet developed the need to fear God or the knowledge of evil to shun it. Yet, after their fall, they learned what evil was and obviously developed a fear for God because they hid from Him.

Because of their actions, the rules of the battle were laid out for the struggle that Adam's and Eve's souls and other souls would have with Satan. In essence, Satan had gained the confidence and a sense of power to battle for souls. He also had an advantage that God allowed him to have. It was the act of deception and man's freewill. Prior to souls taking abode in mankind, souls had not been exposed to either. Nevertheless, he was not given the power for total defeat. He could only strike from below, there was power from above to bruise his head and defeat him. Yet, he would always be striking at the feet trying to draw souls away from God. However, God decreed that he would be defeated by Christ with the statement; He shall bruise your head which predicts the final defeat of Satan through Jesus Christ's redemptive work on the cross. His act of deception gave him a sense of power, but also sealed his final defeat through Jesus Christ. Two example of his weakness to Christ are the failure of Satan to tempt Christ when Christ fasted in the wilderness and Christ's continuation toward the ultimate defeat that sealed our redemption through Christ's human ability to refrain from sin and His divine resurrection.

From here we will begin our journey towards the cross by looking at familiar bible stories. From the stories, we will see how God is laying the foundation for His plan of salvation and at the same time teaching mankind the type of relationship that He desires for man to have with Him. Finally as we approach closer to the cross, we will see Jesus making the teaching clear. His act on the cross and more importantly, His act of resurrection culminated God's plan.

We will look at the story of Cain and Abel to begin our journey and to show how God began to teach mankind soon after the creation and Adam and Eve's fall the importance of controlling our emotions and if we do not how they can lead to sin. As a side note, we also see God first defining murder as sin.

Cain & Abel

Cain and Able were Adam's & Eve's first two sons. Most Bible readers are familiar with the story of Cain killing Able. However, God started teaching a lesson to Cain and to mankind before Cain killed Abel. The lesson started when Cain and Abel presented their offering before the Lord. What was the lesson?

Genesis 4:4-8

The Lord looked with favor on Abel and his offering, but on Cain and his offering he did not look with favor. So Cain was very angry, and his face was downcast. Then the Lord said to Cain, "<u>Why are you angry? Why is your face downcast? If you do what is right, will you not be accepted? But if you do not do what is right, sin is crouching at your door; it desires to have you, but you must rule over it.</u>" Now Cain said to his brother Abel, "Let's go out to the field." While they were in the field, Cain attacked his brother Abel and killed him.

God Addresses Emotions - Anger

This is the first time that the emotion of anger is presented and God talks about it in relationship to sin. After its presentation, God recognizes anger in Cain and addresses it and instructs him on how it can bring about sin. Shortly after that, we read that Cain kills Abel. In addition to God talking about anger, God talks about righteousness and sin. God points out also the relationship of right and wrong to sin. He says if right isn't done, then it opens up the door to sin. In essence, it was wrong for Cain to become angry, but it wasn't a sin. It was Cain's lack of control of his anger that led to the sin of killing Abel. This wasn't just a lesson to Cain, but it was a lesson to all of us. It served two purposes. First it described what Cain's and Abel's parents had done to all mankind by their uncontrolled desire for pleasure, and wisdom as we read above in Genesis 2:17-18; excerpted here. (*… the woman saw that the tree was good for food, and that it was pleasant to the eyes, and a tree to be desired to make one wise, she took of the fruit thereof, and did eat,…*). The knowledge of good and evil brought about a responsibility to utilize it correctly. God made it clear that righteous keeps us a way from sinning. Unrighteous opens the door to sin.

God warned Cain about not controlling his emotion of anger and at the same time conveyed the same message to future generations. Just as Cain's lack of control opened the door for his sinful act of murder against his brother; anger can open the door to sin for each of us. Secondly, God's warning to Cain brought the responsibility of wrong doing and sin down to an individual personal level and indicated that it was something that was going to be there for each to fight against. We must strive to live right, because we are weakened when we do not and must fight harder against falling into more sin when living on the threshold.

After Cain and Abel, Adam and Eve had another son by the name of Seth. Seth was the first in the descendants of Adam down to Noah about which we referenced before in regards to the messianic statement concerning the coming of Christ.

Noah and the Ark

Another familiar story that God used to continue His teaching was the story of Norah. This story involves God beginning His teaching on faith. Because Noah was righteous and faithful to God, God spared him and all mankind because of his faithfulness. Later, we will see where all mankind will have an opportunity to be saved from another man's act of faith. We will also see how God used him to demonstrate what He was going to do to bring salvation. Another interesting point to note is that Noah's name ended the important message about the savior of mankind found in the meaning of the names of Adam and his descendants down to Noah, that we talked about earlier. In addition, we see God making His first covenant with man solely based on God's love for mankind's souls. Genesis 6:17-21, 17 *And behold, I Myself am bringing floodwaters on the earth, to destroy from under heaven all flesh in which is the breath of life; everything that is on the earth shall die. 18 But I will establish My covenant with you; and you shall go into the ark-you, your sons, your wife, and your sons' wives with you. 19 And of every living thing of all flesh you shall bring two of every sort into the ark, to keep them alive with you; they shall be male and female. 20 Of the birds after their kind, of animals after their kind, and of every creeping thing of the earth after its kind, two of every kind will come to you to keep them alive. 21 And you shall take for yourself of all food that is eaten, and you shall gather it to yourself; and it shall be food for you and for them."*

Later, we will see a similar situation where God made an unconditional covenant with another man who was faithful to Him and through remnants of this covenant; all mankind was given the opportunity to be saved. I don't believe that it is just coincidental that all of these seemingly slight incidents come together as they do. To me, there is a connection and a powerful suggestion in them. The lesson is that God showed the weight of having faith in Him and, at the same time gave some very important hints about His plans for the future of mankind' souls journey back to Him.

Chapter IV

ABRAM & SARAI (ABRAHAM & SARAH)

God continued his teaching and the development of His plan for man through His call of Abram. God called Abram and made a promise to Abram. In Geneses 12, we are not given a reason why he had chosen Abram. We only read in Geneses 12: 1-3 that, The Lord had said to Abram, *"Go from your country, your people and your father's household to the land I will show you. "I will make you into a great nation, and I will bless you; I will make your name great, and you will be a blessing. I will bless those who bless you, and whoever curses you I will curse; and all peoples on earth will be blessed through you."*

We see that Abram, who was seventy five years old at the time, gathered all his belonging and took his family and relatives with him and went as the Lord told him to do and arrived in the land of Canaan. This was the land that Abram's father, Terah, was initially going with him, but all stopped in Harran and stayed there until he died at the age of two hundred and five.

Abram was in the land where God had told him to go and a famine occurred. Abram went to live in Egypt for a while because of the famine but feared that he would be killed because his wife Sarai was so beautiful that the men would kill him and take her. Abram told Sarai to tell everyone she was his sister. The Pharaoh took her in as his wife and God allowed sickness to break out in his household. The Pharaoh realized that God was punishing him because of Sarai being Abram's wife and sent them away. However, Abram had amassed great wealth by this time and left with all of his possessions. Here is a hint to the role Egypt, diseases and a Pharaoh would play in sending God's faithful out of Egypt with all their possessions.

God's Unconditional Covenant with Abram

However, God was not through with Abram and Sarai. He still had other plans for their lives that tied to the initial promise that He had made Abram. Abram, his family and Lot left Egypt and they split because the land would not support both of their possessions. Lot moved toward Sodom and Gomorrah and later was taken captive. Abram gathered his men and rescued Lot and received a blessing from Melchizedek. After this, Abram had a vision and God told Abram *"Do not be afraid, Abram. I am your shield, your very great reward."* Abram questioned God about what He could give him since he was childless and his servant would be his heir. In verses four and five, God assured Abram that his heir would be of his own flesh and blood and he would have so many offspring that he wouldn't be able to count them. Later, in Geneses 15:17-21, God sealed His covenant with Abram by passing between the halves of two carcasses. *When the sun had set and darkness had fallen, a smoking firepot with a blazing torch appeared and passed between the pieces. On that day the Lord made a covenant with Abram and said, "To your descendants I give this land, from the Wadi of Egypt to the great river, the Euphrates-the land of the Kenites, Kenizzites, Kadmonites, Hittites, Perizzites, Rephaites, Amorites, Canaanites, Girgashites and Jebusites."* God had made an unconditional covenant with Abram and promised him that his heir would be of his flesh and blood and He would give them the land specified. The covenant was unconditional because only God passes between the two halves. Abram was not required to seal the covenant.

Sarai's Impatience

As time went on Abram still did not have a child and Sarai decided to fix it by giving her slave Hagar to Abram to bear a child. Abram knew that God had told him that he would have an heir of his own flesh. However, he allowed Sarai to persuade him to act differently; his actions in agreeing to go alone with Sari assumed that God needed help to carry out His plan. The lessons that God shows us from their action are many as we will see later. However, several things in the story were a repeat of some of the emotions that occurred with Cain toward Abel which God warned against. Because of the way Sarai went about trying to help God give Abram an heir by providing him with her handmaiden, we see anger; jealousy, rejection, and revenge develop between Sari and Hagar.

God Shows Compassion for Hagar

We also see God's compassion for Hagar who was brought into the situation not by her own desires. She was a slave that did not have a choice in the matter. When she chose to run away, she was told to return and to submit herself to Sarai although she was being abused, but God had her back. He was going to bless her descendants because of her obedience.

Hagar birthed Abram a son and he was named Ishmael as the angel of the Lord had directed Hagar. Abram was eighty six years old at the time of Ishmael's birth. By the time Abram was ninety nine years old, Sarai still had not given him a son, but something happened. The lord appeared before Abram and reaffirmed His earlier covenant but added the rite of circumcision to it.

The Covenant of Circumcision

In addition, God changed his name from Abram to Abraham, changed Sarai name to Sarah, and promised that Sarah would give Abraham a child.

Abram name change: Geneses 17:3-8, *"Then Abram fell on his face, and God talked with him, saying: "As for Me, behold, My covenant is with you, and you shall be a father of many nations. No longer shall your name be called Abram, but your name shall be Abraham; for I have made you a father of many nations. I will make you exceedingly fruitful; and I will make nations of you, and kings shall come from you. And I will establish My covenant between Me and you and your descendants after you in their generations, for an everlasting covenant, to be God to you and your descendants after you."*

Sarai's name change: Geneses 17:15-21 states, *"God also said to Abraham, "As for Sarai your wife, you are no longer to call her Sarai; her name will be Sarah. I will bless her and will surely give you a son by her. I will bless her so that she will be the mother of nations; kings of peoples will come from her." Abraham fell facedown; he laughed and said to himself, "Will a son be born to a man a hundred years old? Will Sarah bear a child at the age of ninety?" And Abraham said to God, "If only Ishmael might live under your blessing!"*

God Specifically tells Abraham that Sarah will bear him a Son

Then God said, "Yes, but your wife Sarah will bear you a son, and you will call him Isaac. I will establish my covenant with him as an everlasting covenant for his descendants after him. And as for Ishmael, I have heard you: I will surely bless him; I will make him fruitful and will greatly increase his numbers. He will be the father of twelve rulers, and I will make him into a great nation. But my covenant I will establish with Isaac, whom Sarah will bear to you by this time next year."

The story of Abraham and Sarah was a bedrock event in God's developing plan of restoration for man. It was a continuation of an educational process that God had started providing for man to come to an understanding of His master plan and who He is. In these verses we see the foundation laid for Christ in the promise of establishing an everlasting covenant with Isaac. From Hagar, we learn that God honors and blesses obedience. We already know from Adam and Eve that God punishes disobedience.

There is another hint I believe that we miss in this story and the actions God took with Abram and Sarai. Before covenanting with them, He changed their names. In essence they were no longer to be who they were prior to the covenant. I believe this may be a forerunning representation of the change that Christ would usher in and the Holy Spirit would bring about in us after accepting Christ in our lives. Paul put it this way. 2 Corinthians 5:17 (NKJV), *"Therefore, if anyone is in Christ, he is a new creation; old things have passed away; behold, all things have become new."*

Abraham & Isaac - the Salvation Plan

We continue to see hints that God provided for us in the Old Testament to let us know what was coming from Him. Let's look at God's conversation with Abraham concerning his only son Isaac whom God had given him and Sarah as fulfilment of His covenant with them.

> *Genesis 17:19: But God replied, "No Sarah, your wife, will give birth to a son for you. You will name him Isaac, and I will confirm my covenant with him and his descendants as an everlasting covenant."*

Genesis 22: 2: "Take your son, your only son - yes,
Isaac, whom you love so much and go to the land of
Moriah. Go and sacrifice him as a burnt offering on one
of the mountains, which I will show you."

Genesis 22: 7-8: "... We have the fire and the wood,"
the boy said, "but where is the sheep for the burnt
offering? God will provide a sheep for the burnt
offering, my son,"...

God asked Abraham to sacrifice his only son by Sarah to Him. Abraham started forth with the sacrifice but God stopped him. Abraham's faith that God would provide a substitute was an indication that God was going to provide a substitute for mankind's sin if mankind had the faith to believe. Also, notice what God said to Abraham concerning Isaac. God said, *"Take your son, your only son, yes, Isaac, whom you love so much."* We know that Abraham had another son, Ishmael by Hagar the Egyptian servant of Sarah, but God said to Abraham your only son. It was their only son that God had given him and Sarah when she was past her child bearing age. I believe that God specified "your only son whom you love so much" because it was a sign that it was what God was going to do for mankind. He was going to take His only Son who He had given to mankind to be a sacrifice for mankind's sin. It was not just a sign of what He was going to do, but it was also a sign of the significance of what it should mean to mankind. God's gift of His son was to show us how much He loved and loves us and so we would know the real meaning of love and His love for us.

God did not withhold His only son. He provided Christ as a substitute for our sin as God provided a sheep for Abraham as a substitute for Isaac. God loved our souls so much that He was willing to make the sacrifice of giving up His Son in order to give us the opportunity to choose to return to Him.

Genesis 22:15-18 reads, *The angel of the Lord called to Abraham from heaven a second time and said, "I swear by myself, declares the Lord, that because you have done this and have not withheld your son, your only son, I will surely bless you and make your descendants as numerous as the stars in the sky and as the sand on the seashore. Your descendants will take possession of the cities of their enemies, and through your offspring all nations on earth will be blessed, because you have obeyed me."*

When we examine the verses where the angel called Abraham to stop from slaying Isaac, we see what God said why He asked Abraham to do it in the first place. In a sense, God was testing Abraham. Abraham act of obedience and willingness to offer his son became the reason for all nations' blessings. We can see that God was revealing more and more of His master plan and was continuing to lay the foundation to bring it to fruition.

Abraham Seeks a Wife for Isaac

Later after Sarah's death, Abraham had his servant go back to his homeland to find a wife for his son Isaac. He went and found Rebekah and brought her back and Isaac and Rebekah were married.

An Indication of God's Intimate Relationship

One thing that stood out in the story of the servant going to get Rebekah was what he did to insure that she was the right person. He began to pray to God and in retelling the story to Rebekah's family, he made the statement that before he finished his prayer in his heart, God answered it. It was the first time it was mentioned about God answering prayers in our hearts. We can see God's plan developing even more. We begin to get a better picture of the intimate relationship God desired for us to have with Him. In addition from the story, we can begin to see how God was going to continue His promise to Abraham and Isaac. We can surmise that marriage is going to bring about more children to insure the fulfilment of the covenant God made with Abraham.

Isaac and Rebekah

Rebekah did not become pregnant until Isaac prayed and asked God for a child, and we see again God providing a childless woman birth to a child and in this case, twins. Could God have been giving an indication about what He was going to do later on with a virgin by giving childless women children? After Rebekah becomes pregnant, she learned from God that she was going to have twins and that they represented two nations. In addition, the older would serve the younger. Their names were Esau and Jacob and they grew up having different interests. Esau, the oldest, liked hunting and was favored by Isaac while Jacob preferred staying in and was favored by Rebekah. After the birth of Esau and Jacob, a famine came to the land but the Lord told Isaac to stay in the land where He told him and he would be blessed. Isaac did as the Lord told him.

Later after Isaac became old and blind, he was tricked by Rebekah in giving his younger son Jacob, Esau's blessings. Esau swore to kill Jacob so Rebekah sent Jacob away from Esau to her relative to get a wife.

Jacob

God Confirms to Jacob the Covenant

On the way, Jacob had a dream where God confirmed the covenant to Jacob that He had made first to Abraham and also to Isaac. Again we see God building on and teaching about his master plan. In addition, we see the first time a tenth of giving is mentioned. Jacob made a vow to God that he would give God a tenth of everything God gave him, if God would be with him, look over him and return him safely home.

Rachel and Leah

Finally Jacob arrived at his destination and found his relatives. He first met Rachel, Laban's younger daughter, at the well and she took him home to meet his uncle. Jacob made an agreement with Laban to work seven years for Rachel's hand in marriage but after the seven years and after the marriage celebration, Laban sent his older daughter, Leah to Jacob and Jacob unknowingly made love to her. The next morning, he discovered what happened and confronted Laban. Laban agreed to give him Rachel if he finished out the bridal week with Leah and work for another seven years. Jacob did, received Rachel and made love to her and finished out the seven years.

Jacob's Eleven Sons

Jacob loved Rachel more than Leah and again we see God's compassion for the rejected. After God saw that Leah was not loved, He stepped in and enabled Leah to conceive four times for four sons. They were named Reuben, Simeon, Levi and Judah. She gave a reason for the name chosen for each one. Reuben was "because the Lord has seen my misery" Reuben sounds like the Hebrew for he has seen my misery but the name means see, a son. Simeon was, "because the Lord heard that I am not loved". Levi was, "because now my husband will become attached to me". Was God again conveying a message to man? Maybe God was letting man know, behold a son (Ruben), God's Son Jesus, who will mend the break because He had seen man's misery (Ruben) since breaking the spiritual connection with Him and know that man feels unloved (Simeon), but when My Son comes He will attach (Levi) you back to me and then you will praise (Judah) me. The Bible then says after she had Judah, she stopped having children. I believe that God inspired the writer to break up Leah's child bearing with Jacob at that point because He was giving man a message. It was a similar message He had given in the meaning of the names of Adam's descendants down to Noah.

As we continue, we will see that God did not stop with Leah's four sons. Because of jealousy we see as in the case of Cain and Abel, and Sari and Hagar that Rachel reacted to it. She gave her servant Bilhah to Jacob to have children for her. Again we see a repeat of situations from the emotion of jealousy caused by anger. There were two sons, Dan and Naphtali, born to Jacob by Bilhah. Again jealousy occurred and Leah, Rachel's sister, gave her servant Zilpah to Jacob so he could sleep with her and have children for Leah. There were two more sons from this arrangement. They were Gad and Asher.

After this, Rachel agreed to allow Leah to sleep with Jacob again for some food Leah's son had. Leah conceived two more times and had two more sons by Jacob. They were Issachar and Zebulun.

Finally, Rachel gave birth to a son. Rachel named him Joseph and said, "The Lord has taken away my disgrace. May He add to me another son." Joseph's name means, "may God add or give increase." At this point, Jacob has eleven sons. The first four by Leah, two by Rachel servant Bilhah, two by Leah's servant Zilpah, two more by Leah, and one by Rachel.

Jacob and Laban

We can see that the story of God's love for us was continuing to be written although no one really knew it. We are now on the forefront of the beginning of the nation of Israel. After Joseph was born, Jacob accumulated many possessions of animals through an agreement with Laban in spite of Laban trying to cheat him. God tells Jacob to go back to his home land. Jacob sets out for his homeland without telling Laban and Laban pursues him, overtakes him but does him no harm because God warns Laban and tells him not to do so. A covenant is made between Jacob and Laban and Laban returns home. Now, Jacob faces another problem by the name of Esau, Jacob's betrayed brother. Jacob makes preparation to meet Esau, but is fearful of what Esau is going to do to him after receiving report that Esau is on his way to meet him with four hundred men. Part of Jacob's preparation leaves him alone on the other side of the Jordan after sending everyone else over.

Jacob wrestles with God

While there alone, we see Jacob struggled with a man and Jacob didn't let him go until he blessed him. The blessing Jacob received was the changing of his name from Jacob to Israel. The man told him "Your name will no longer be Jacob, but Israel, because you have struggled with God and with humans and have overcome." In the struggle the man touched Jacob's hip at its socket and wrenched it. Let's examine this story more closely. Was it really God that Jacob was physically wrestling with? The story really disputes that it was. Surely God had the power to defeat Jacob in a wrestling match. As we analyze the statement that the man said more closely, we see two entities mentioned, they were God and mankind. It appears to me that Jacob was wrestling with himself and with God. He was wrestling with God to the extent that he was confused and wanted God to give him an answer or assurance that everything was going to be okay between him and Esau. He was wrestling with himself because he knew that he had wronged Esau, but was now repentant for it. Jacob was not going to stop praying to God and asking him for whatever he needed until God gave him an answer. During the struggle, Jacob discovered who he really was. God blessed him by giving him the name of Israel, the nation of which he would be the father. Whether he physically wrestled with a man or not, is the not the most important lesson from his experience. He did not let go of God until he received the blessing he desired. It was an allnight struggle, in which he was afflicted from the struggle, but in the end, he received his blessing. Whether Jacob really understood his blessing I do not know, but he knew for sure God had blessed him. The Bible says, *"So Jacob called the place Peniel (face of God) saying, "It is because I saw God face to face, and yet my life was spared."* Later when we talk about when Jacob met Esau, we will see that Jacobs tells us through his conversation about what part of his wrestling was about.

Jacob and Esau Face to Face

After this experience, Jacob joined Rachel and the others and saw Esau coming with four hundred men. When Esau saw Jacob he ran toward him and hugged him. He refused the gifts that Jacob had sent ahead of his arrival but Jacob insisted that he keep them. *"No, please!" said Jacob. "If I have found favor in your eyes, accept this gift from me. For to see your face is like seeing the face of God, now that you have received me favorably."* We see that the image that came to Jacobs mind when he saw Esau was him wrestling with God through the night. This I believe is a confirmation that part of Jacob's struggle was his guilt for what he had done to Esau many years before. Now he knew that God and Esau had vindicated him for his actions. God had received him favorably after struggling in anguish with God through the night and Esau had forgiven him and received him favorably.

Jacob's daughter Dinah Defiled & Revenged

After meeting Esau, Jacobs does not go with Esau as Esau wants, but tells him he will come later because he has to take it slow because of the young animals and women and children. In the meantime, Jacob camps outside of the city of Shechem in Canaan. His daughter by Leah went out to visit the women of the land and was raped by Shechem's son of Hamor the Hivite, the ruler of that area. He fell in love with her and wanted to marry her. Hamor went to Jacob and asked permission for his son to marry her. Jacob's son and Jacob knew that Dinah had been defiled. Jacob's son told Hamor the only way his son could marry their sister was that all the men in the city must be circumcised. Hamor agreed and the men went along with it. All the men were circumcised and after three days when they were in pain doing the healing process, two of Jacob's sons, Simeon and Levi, Dinah's brothers killed all the men and took Dinah from Schechem house. Later the other sons took all the women, children and all valuables from the city. Jacob was upset with Simeon and Levi and told them, *"You have brought trouble on me by making me obnoxious to the Canaanites and Perizzites, the people living in this land. We are few in number, and if they join forces against me and attack me, I and my household will be destroyed."*

After this God told Jacob to go to Bethel and build an altar there to God. Jacob had his household and all who were with him to get rid of all foreign gods, purify themselves and change clothes. They all arrived in Bethel and Jacob built the altar. Later, God appeared to him again and blessed him. God said to him, *"Your name is Jacob, but you will no longer be called Jacob; your name will be Israel."* So he named him Israel.

And God said to him, "I am God Almighty; be fruitful and increase in number. A nation and a community of nations will come from you, and kings will be among your descendants. The land I gave to Abraham and Isaac I also give to you, and I will give this land to your descendants after you." Then God went up from him at the place where he had talked with him. Jacob called the place where God had talked with him Bethel. *(House of God)*

After this, Jacob and the others left Bethel and some distance from Ephrath, Rachel who was pregnant with Jacob's son started to give birth, but had difficulty and died after the child was born. Just before she died, she named him Ben-Oni *(son of my trouble)*. However, Jacob named him Benjamin *(Son of my right hand)*

Jacob went home to his father Isaac, and at the age of one hundred eighty Isaac died. Esau and Jacob buried him.

God Completes a Phase of His Plan

With the birth of Benjamin, God completed the formation of the basic nation of Israel. Jacob's twelve sons would be the twelve tribes of the nation of Israel.

God had laid the foundation for the nation that He was going to use to teach all mankind who He was and to share His master plan. As we continue, we are going to see how God worked through what seemed to be disaster, to show his grace, mercy and awesome power and to insure that His master plan would come to fruition.

Joseph

Joseph's Dreams and Joseph is Sold

Joseph had two dreams and each implied that his brothers would be bowing down to him. His brothers already hated Joseph because his father favored him and had given him a coat of many colors. The dreams only increased their hatred toward him. Jacob sent Joseph to see about his brothers who were grazing their sheep near Shechem. When Joseph got there his brothers were not there, but a man told him they had gone to Dothan. Joseph went to Dothan and his brothers saw him coming. They plotted to kill him, but Ruben told them not to kill him. Later they sold him to some Ishmaelite for twenty shekels of silver who took him to Egypt. In Egypt Joseph is sold to Potiphar, one of Pharaoh's officials, the captain of the guard.

Meanwhile, Ruben went to the cistern where Joseph had initially been thrown for the purpose of rescuing him. When he went to his brothers after not finding Joseph in the cistern, his brothers dipped Joseph coat into blood and took it to their father to identify it. Jacob identified the coat as Joseph's and assumed that he had been torn to pieces and devoured by a wild animal. Jacob went into a deep mourning.

Joseph in Egypt

In Egypt, God was with Joseph and Joseph found favor with Potiphar and Potiphar entrusted everything to Joseph's management. Joseph was handsome and well built. Potiphar wife wanted Joseph to sleep with her but Joseph refused. She falsely accused Joseph of trying to do so and Potiphar threw Joseph in jail. But again God stepped in and continued His plan for Joseph. The prison warden took a liking to Joseph and put Joseph over all the other prisoners and made him responsible for all that was done there.

The Cupbearer and the Baker's Dreams

Although, Joseph was in prison, God's plan was still unfolding. God knew what he had planned for Joseph. Joseph just had to be patient and wait for God to work His plan. Part of God's plan involved the king's cupbearer and baker. Both had been put into prison where Joseph was for offending the king in some manner. While there, each had different dreams the same night. Joseph interpreted the dreams. The cupbearer was restored back to his position with the king as Joseph had said and the baker was killed in the manner Joseph had said. Joseph told the cupbearer to remember him to the king when he returned to his position. The cupbearer forgot Joseph until the king had two dreams no one else could interpret. Joseph was brought to the king and God interpret the dreams through Joseph.

The dream's interpretations were that Egypt would have seven prosperous years and seven years of famine. Joseph suggested that the king find a responsible person to put in charge of stockpiling food for the seven years of famine that would follow the prosperous years. Since Joseph was the only one able to interpret the dreams, the king placed Joseph over everything in Egypt, and made him only second to himself.

Joseph's Brothers go to Egypt

The seven prosperous years came and went, and the seven years of famine started. The famine did not just affect Egypt but was everywhere including Joseph's homeland of Canaan. When Joseph brothers and Father heard there was grain in Egypt, ten of Joseph brothers went to Egypt to purchase food. They arrived in Egypt and went before Joseph who recognized them, but they did not recognize him. Joseph accused them of being spies to accomplish the goal of getting his younger brother there in Egypt. He held one of the brothers there and told the others to go and get the younger brother so it would verify their story; and after they return, he would let the other brother go. The brothers went back home and told Israel what happened. Jacob did not want to send his younger son, Benjamin, with them. Eventually, after running out of food, he agrees. They returned to Egypt with their younger brother. After Joseph made them squirm a while, he finally revealed who he was. Joseph told them what they did was part of God's plan. He said to his brothers, *"And now, do not be distressed and do not be angry with yourselves for selling me here, because it was to save lives that God sent me ahead of you." Genesis 45:5* Although Joseph could see that what happened to him was part of God's plan, yet, he did not know the master plan that God was implementing.

Joseph's Father goes to Egypt

After revealing himself to his brothers, he told them to go and get their father and all of their families and come back to Egypt. He showered them with goods and provided carts for their father, the children and women. After going back to get their families, they returned to Egypt with their families and their father and were given land. Before Israel decided to go to Egypt, the lord told him, "I am God, the God of your father," he said. *"Do not be afraid to go down to Egypt, for I will make you into a great nation there. I will go down to Egypt with you, and I will surely bring you back again. Genesis 46:3-4*

We see that it appears that God only revealed part of His plan to Israel. Later when Jacob/Israel blesses his sons, we see that his blessings are prophetic. We can now see the building blocks of the nation of Israel being laid. God's pronouncement to Abram that his descendants would be enslaved in a foreign land for four hundred years was being prepared. We can see the progression of God's plan that started with the naming of Adam and his descendants, continuing to the stories of Abram and Sarai and on up to Joseph being sold to end up in Egypt. God was stepping through His plan and showing His love along the way moving toward His ultimate show of love by giving His only begotten son for our redemption.

Israel Blesses His Son and Dies

After Joseph's family arrived and settled in Egypt, Israel grew older and before he died he blessed Joseph's two sons, Manasseh and Ephraim. In doing so he placed his right hand on Ephraim's head and his left hand on Manasseh's head, putting the younger Ephraim ahead of Manasseh. He also blessed his sons and gave each the blessing that was appropriate to them. His blessing is found in Genesis 49. His blessings were really prophecies about each of his sons. At the very beginning of Jacob/Israel blessings, he showed that he realized that the change of his name was more than just a name change. It was a significant blessing and a change in him. In Genesis 49:2 he called his sons together and said, *"Assemble and listen, sons of Jacob; listen to your father Israel."* He made a distinction between himself as Jacob and himself as Israel. His sons were of Jacobs, but he was their father as Israel. His prophecies during his son's blessing and the distinction between his names, showed that God had not only given him a new name, but had given him a revelation of at least part of His plan. Jacob/Israel died and Joseph buried him and later reassured his brothers that they did not have to fear reprisal from him.

Israel the Nation in Egypt

The stage had been set for the nation of Israel to stay and grow in Egypt. They grew so large that the new king enslaved them. The Israelites were in Egypt and enslaved for some four hundred years before they finally left. God had made a way for them to get to Egypt and to grow into a nation, and He made a way for them to leave Egypt. Many are familiar with the story of the Exodus, but only a few see that the miracles that God performed for the Israelites, started way before they were in Egypt as a nation.

The point of this long discussion through the book of Genesis was to show that God's progression of His plan for mankind's salvation started from the beginning and to show how God laid the foundation for it. Although many people were part of God's plan, they did not know they were part of it or knew the role they played. It also showed that even things in God's plan may not happen immediately, yet His word holds through generations. It was four hundred years that passed before God took the next major step in His plan. Even in taking this step, God took His time in setting it up. Just as God had saved Joseph and used him in His plan, He saved Moses and used him. Just as Joseph did, Moses had to go through some hardships even after his life as a baby had been saved and he was reared in royalty. He had to flee from Pharaoh after killing an Egyptian.

As we look at Scripture closely, we see God's development of His plan of salvation. We have seen in our discussion how God set up the development of the nation of Israel from the twelve sons of Jacobs to a multitude. The Bible says in Exodus 1:6-7, *"Now Joseph and all his brothers and all that generation died, but the Israelites were exceedingly fruitful; they multiplied greatly, increased in numbers and became so numerous that the land was filled with them."* We know the roles the nation of Israel played in the revealing and the development of God's plan. The roles were diverse but each role was important in showing and the development of the type of relationship God desired for mankind. There were highs and lows in the relationship the nation had with God. Nevertheless, God never left the nation completely. There were periods that they pushed God away, but realized that they could not make it without Him and they repented and God became active in their lives again. Even during these times, God never stopped loving them and implementing His plan of redemption. These were teaching moments for the people.

Now let's look at some of the moments in the life of Israel where God continued to develop his plan. We left off with the multitude of Israel's descendants in Egypt. The king of Egypt enslaved them and oppressed them but they kept multiplying. Finally the king ordered that all new born male children be killed.

Chapter V

MOSES

Moses was one of the new born babies that would have been killed, but God stepped in and rescued and fixed it that he would be raised in the king's palace. To appreciate the irony here, one must really think about what God did. The king gave the orders to kill all the babies, but his daughter ended up saving one of the babies who God would use to liberate all of His chosen people. Moses later killed an Egyptian for mistreating a Hebrew and fled to Midian. There he met Zipporah, married her and had a son named Gershom. In the meantime, the king of Egypt died and the burden continued to increase on the Israelites. They cried out to God and He heard their plea for help. The Bible says, *"God heard their groaning and he remembered his covenant with Abraham, with Isaac and with Jacob."*

Moses while tending his father-in law Jethro's flock took them to Horeb, the mountain of God. There God called to him. When Moses went to investigate a burning bush that wasn't being consumed by the fire, God told Moses who He was and gave Moses his mission. In doing so, God told him that He would have to convince Pharaoh to let the Israelites go and eventually Pharaoh would. We see that God already knew the outcome of what would happen. As far as

God was concerned, it was done. Moses and the Israelites just had to carry out what God had already laid out. God wasn't hindered by the time it was going to take to achieve it, but Moses and the Israelites were. However, they were just components of the plan that God had already prepared that would occur. Pharaoh was a component of it also and God knew his reactions ahead of time. Even when Pharaoh had the mind to act one way, God hardened his heart to make him act another way. God was teaching mankind who He was and the power He had. It was necessary for mankind to come to the realization that God had the power to destroy all, yet the heart and the desire to save those who call on Him.

Everything that we've discussed thus far about God's actions, was part of God's plan to bring awareness to the people at that time about who He was. We saw that He chose a people and developed them into a nation. In the process, He laid the foundation for His master plan of salvation. As we continue to follow this nation, we will see Him working with them to help them understand and develop the type of relationship He desired for them and all mankind to have with Him. God desired for them and all mankind to know Him personally and intimately the way He knows us. We have seen the start of God working through chosen individuals to first develop the nation. We will see Him continue to work through individuals to teach them who He is and what He expects of them. We will see this process start with Moses. We will continue to follow that teaching process and see how much they had learned by the time Christ came.

Moses Obeys

After God gave Moses his mission and told Moses what to do and what would happen, Moses was reluctant to go and told God about his inability to speak plainly. God assured him that He would take care of the problem, but Moses still wanted someone to go with him. God told him Aaron his brother would go with him. One of the things God revealed to Moses was that He would harden Pharaoh's heart and

Pharaoh would not let the people go. *Exodus 4:21-23, The Lord said to Moses, "When you return to Egypt, see that you perform before Pharaoh all the wonders I have given you the power to do. But I will harden his heart so that he will not let the people go. Then say to Pharaoh, 'This is what the Lord says: Israel is my firstborn son, and I told you, "Let my son go, so he may worship me." But you refused to let him go; so I will kill your firstborn son."*

The Purpose of the Plagues

The question may be asked, why did God harden Pharaoh's heart? God was performing more than one act through his actions with the Egyptians. His actions were to teach and show the Israelites and the Egyptians who He was, the power He had and the love He had for His chosen people. He wanted them to know that He was God who had control over all including life and death. Because so many are familiar with the story of the Exodus, I will not go through it in its entirety. However, the ten plagues that God brought upon Egypt, demonstrated to the Egyptians and the Israelites, who God was and His awesome power. Here is a list of the plagues found in Exodus Chapters 7 through 12.

The Plague of Blood

The Plague of Frogs

The Plague of Gnats

The Plague of Flies

The Plague on Livestock

The Plague of Boils

The Plague of Hail

The Plague of Locusts

The Plague of Darkness

The Plague on the Firstborn

Just before the plague of the hail, God told Pharaoh the reason that he was bringing the plagues on him. It is below. It is also the reason that God hardened Pharaoh's heart so that the plagues would be brought against Egypt. God was teaching and showing the Israelites and all who were to follow, His might.

Exodus 9:15-16, For by now I could have stretched out my hand and struck you and your people with a plague that would have wiped you off the earth. But I have raised you up for this very purpose, that I might show you my power and that my name might be proclaimed in all the earth.

The Tenth Plague on the First born

The last plague on the firstborn had more significance than many may realize. It was a special message that God was delivering through it. We will examine it closer.

Exodus 12: 12-13 (NLT) On that night I will pass through the land of Egypt and strike down every firstborn son and firstborn male animal in the land of Egypt. I will execute judgment against all the gods of Egypt, for I am the Lord! But the blood on your doorposts will serve as a sign, marking the houses where you are staying. When I see the blood, I will pass over you. This plague of death will not touch you when I strike the land of Egypt.

The significance of this plague was another hint to mankind of what God's plan of salvation was. It was an indication of what God would later do to bring salvation. God's firstborn Son's blood would cause the death angel that was and is over mankind, brought on by Adam and Eve's sin, to pass over those beneath His Son's blood.

Pharaoh Lets the People Go and God's Promise to Abram Fulfilled

Finally after the last plague, of the firstborn child dying, Pharaoh decided to let the people go. Not only did he let them go but he fulfilled the promise God had given Abram. Genesis 15:13-14, *Then the Lord said to him, "Know for certain that for four hundred years your descendants will be strangers in a country not their own and that they will be enslaved and mistreated there. But I will punish the nation they serve as slaves, and afterward they will come out with great possessions.*

After four hundred years, the promise to Abram was fulfilled just as God had promised. *Exodus 12: 33-36, The Egyptians urged the people to hurry and leave the country. "For otherwise," they said, "we will all die!" So the people took their dough before the yeast was added, and carried it on their shoulders in kneading troughs wrapped in clothing. The Israelites did as Moses instructed and asked the Egyptians for articles of silver and gold and for clothing. The Lord had made the Egyptians favorably disposed toward the people, and they gave them what they asked for; so they plundered the Egyptians.*

Pharaoh Pursued the Israelites, God is Glorified

However, God was not through letting the Egyptians know who He was and His power. Pharaoh had let the people go, but God wanted them to really know who He was and His power. So God hardened Pharaoh's heart and he and the people of Egypt changed their minds about letting the Israelites go. This was done as a teaching lesson to the Egyptians. God told Moses in Exodus 14:3-4, *"Pharaoh will think, 'The Israelites are wandering around the land in confusion, hemmed in by the desert.' And I will harden Pharaoh's heart, and he will pursue them. But I will gain glory for myself through Pharaoh and all his army, and the Egyptians will know that I am the Lord."*

So Pharaoh pursued the Israelites just as God had told Moses he would, and the result was that all of the Egyptians who pursued the Israelites into the parted sea were killed. We can see again God teaching His people to trust Him. He did this by allowing them to be placed into what seemed to be an inescapable situation, and then He came to their rescue.

The lesson was not just meant for the Israelites His chosen people, but also for the Egyptians who were not His chosen people. It was meant for the Israelites to build their faith and for the Egyptians so they would know who God was. In our lives as believers, we sometime find ourselves in inescapable situations. We can take heart from the lesson God taught the Israelites that when we find ourselves backed up against an inescapable situation; trust God because He is able to bring us out. When He does, we must share what He did so He gets the glory. It's not for God's benefit, but for the benefit of others to come to Him.

God Tests and Develops the Nation

The Israelites crossed the red sea and traveled in the desert of Shur for three days without finding water. When they reached Marah they could not drink the water and they complained. God fixed the problem and also He issued a ruling and instruction for them and put them to the test. Exodus 15: 26, He said, *"If you listen carefully to the Lord your God and do what is right in his eyes, if you pay attention to his commands and keep all his decrees, I will not bring on you any of the diseases I brought on the Egyptians, for I am the Lord, who heals you."* They proceeded to Elim and found drinkable water. They left and went into the Desert of Sin, where they complained about not having food. We see God giving them another test to see if they will obey Him. *Exodus 26:4 Then the Lord said to Moses, "I will rain down bread from heaven for you. The people are to go out each day and gather enough for that day. In this way I will test them and see whether they will follow my instructions.*

God tested the Israelites to see if they would follow His instruction after all they had seen Him do for them. God continued this process with the nation of Israel throughout the Old Testament. However, when God was put to the test, He always delivered for Israel as He promised. God had already proved to Israel that He cared for them and was their protectorate by their deliverance from Egypt. Yet, the people still doubted God. After they left the Desert of Sin and traveled from place to place as God had commanded, they came to Riphidim and no water was there to drink. The people tested God through quarrelling with Moses about not having water. Moses inquired to God about the people's concern. So Exdous 17:5-7 states, *The Lord answered Moses, "Go out in front of the people. Take with you some of the elders of Israel and take in your hand the staff with which you struck the Nile, and go. I will stand there before you by the rock at Horeb. Strike the rock, and water will come out of it for the people to drink." So Moses did this in the sight of the elders of Israel. And he called the place Massah (which means testing) and Meriba (which means quarreling) because the Israelites quarreled and because they tested the Lord saying, "Is the Lord among us or not?"*

God gave the people encouragement and again showed the people His power by providing for them. God continued to come to their rescue even when they did not deserve it because they had turned from Him to embrace Idols. Although God always remained with them, they still suffered at times because of their disobedience. There at Riphidim another significant thing happened in God's plan. We read that the Amalekites attacked the Israelites and God defeated them. God did it by demonstrating visibly that He was with them and controlled the outcome of the battle. He had Moses, Aaron and Hur go to the top of a hill and when Moses held up his hands, the Israelites would win, but whenever he lowered his hands, the Amalekites would win. Aron and Hur had Moses sit on a rock and they took position on each side of him and held up Moses hands. But the point here is not the battle, but who Moses chose to lead the fight and what God told Moses after the battle was won. *Exodous 17:14, Then the Lord said to Moses, "Write this on a scroll as something to be remembered and make sure that Joshua hears it, because I will completely blot out the name of Amalek from under heaven."*

God told Moses to make sure that Joshua heard it. We who know the complete story of the Israelites journey to the promise land know the role that God had for Joshua. This was the first indication that God had a role for Joshua. We know how God had developed His plan to get the Israelites to where they were at Riphidim and even why they were there. In a sense, it was about Joshua getting battle experience and for him to see that God was with him in battle.

Later we read about Moses Father-in-Law, Jethro, coming to him bringing back Moses wife, Zipporah, and sons. Jethro sums up what God's intent was for the Israelites by telling Moses how to do it when Moses was trying to be the Judge for all the people. *Exodus 18:19-20, Listen now to me and I will give you some advice, and may God be with you. You must be the people's representative before God and bring their disputes to him. Teach them his decrees and instructions, and show them the way they are to live and how they are to behave.*

Jethro was telling Moses that the load was too much for him and that he needed to get help to judge the people. However, in the process, he summed up what God's plan for the Israelites as well as for all mankind when he said, "...*show them the way they are to live and how they are to behave.*" God continued to make this point to the Israelites throughout the Old Testament and Christ brought the same message and it was presented in the New Testament. God gave the Israelites the law to show them His desires, but after that He wrote it in men's heart. *Jeremiah 31: 33-34 "But this is the covenant which I will make with the house of Israel after those days," declares the LORD, "I will put My law within them and on their heart I will write it; and I will be their God, and they shall be My people.*

They will not teach again, each man his neighbor and each man his brother, saying, 'Know the LORD,' for they will all know Me, from the least of them to the greatest of them," declares the LORD, "for I will forgive their iniquity, and their sin I will remember no more." …

So Moses took Jethro's advice and chose judges to hear the people complaints, and the ones they could not settle were taken to Moses. On the first day of the third month after the Israelites left Egypt, the Israelites ended up in the Desert of Sinai and camped at the foot of Mount Sinai. Moses went up the mountain and God gave him instructions on what to tell the people about His coming to the mountain to hear God speak with Moses so the people would always put their trust in Moses. *Exodus 19:10-11 And the Lord said to Moses, "Go to the people and consecrate them today and tomorrow. Have them wash their clothes and be ready by the third day, because on that day the Lord will come down on Mount Sinai in the sight of all the people.* So on the third day, God descended on the mountain in an awesome way with smoke, trumpets, fire and shaking of the mountain. Moses went up the mountain and God gave him further instructions. Finally God spoke the Ten Commandments to him and the people heard God speak. We see God directly doing what Jethro had told Moses to do for God, "…*show them the way they are to live and how they are to behave."*

God gave Moses other laws and instructions for the people to follow and told him to write them down. Later Moses went back up the mountain and stayed forty days and forty nights. While Moses was gone, the people lost faith in Moses and seemed to forget that God had brought them out of Egypt. They made an idol calf and began to worship it. God told Moses to go back to the people and that He was going to destroy them. Moses pleaded for their lives and God relinquished. When Moses went down the mountain and witness what the people had done and was doing, he broke the tablets on which

God had written His commandments. *Exodus 32:19 When Moses approached the camp and saw the calf and the dancing, his anger burned and he threw the tablets out of his hands, breaking them to pieces at the foot of the mountain.*

Moses told the people whoever was for the Lord to come to him. The Levites went to his side. He had them to take their sword to others and three thousand were killed. After this, Moses continued talking to God, and God continued leading the people laying out laws and practices that would develop them morally and spiritually into the nation that He desired for them to be. Because of the nature of the people, it was not an overnight task.

God wanted the people to know that He cared for them and wanted to have an intimate relationship with them so he had them build a sanctuary for Him. Before He told Moses to build a sanctuary for him, He told Moses to have the people bring to the tabernacle an offering for Him. However, He only wanted the people to give whose heart led them to give. *Exodus 25:2, The Lord said to Moses, "Tell the Israelites to bring me an offering. You are to receive the offering for me from everyone whose heart prompts them to give….make a sanctuary for me, and I will dwell among them." (Exodus 25:8)*

"Then I will dwell among the Israelites and be their God. They will know that I am the Lord their God, who brought them out of Egypt so that I might dwell among them." (Exodus 29:45-46)

We repeatedly see where God continued teaching the people the type of relationship that was required of them for Him to dwell among them. It was pointing the way to God's ultimate plan here on earth for His Son to dwell among us to usher in the spiritual intimate relationship with each who believes in Him.

A Different Relationship

The coming of Christ would fulfill the prophecies that had been made about His coming. His coming would usher in the beginning of a new type of relationship that man would have with God. Primarily God had dealt with His people directly through the prophets by allowing His Holy Spirit work through them. The birth of Christ would initiate the start of a more intimate and personal relationship; a relationship where all would have a direct connection to God and be empowered by His Holy Spirit.

In Numbers chapter 11, the Israelites complained to Moses about not having meat to eat. Moses took the complaint to God. God said to him in verse 16, *"Bring me seventy of Israel's elders who are known to you as leaders and officials among the people. Have them come to the tent of meeting, that they may stand there with you."* We see the results in verses 21-29 below. However, the result is not the point of why the story is mentioned here. The underlined statement below that Moses made to Joshua's comment is the point. *(Numbers 11: 21-29) But Moses said, "Here I am among six hundred thousand men on foot, and you say, 'I will give them meat to eat for a whole month!' Would they have enough if flocks and herds were slaughtered for them? Would they have enough if all the fish in the sea were caught for them?" The Lord answered Moses, "Is the Lord's arm too short? Now you will see whether or not what I say will come true for you." So Moses went out and told the people what the Lord had said. He brought together seventy of their elders and had them stand around the tent. Then the Lord came down in the cloud and spoke with him, and he took some of the power of the Spirit that was on him and put it on the seventy elders. When the Spirit rested on them, they prophesied - but did not do so again. However, two men, whose names were Eldad and Medad, had remained in the camp. They were listed among the elders, but did not go out to the tent. Yet the Spirit also rested on them, and they prophesied in the camp. A young man ran and told Moses, "Eldad and Medad are prophesying in the camp." Joshua son of Nun, who had been Moses' aide since youth, spoke up and said, "Moses, my lord, stop them!" But Moses replied, "Are you jealous for my sake? I wish that all the Lord's people were prophets and that the Lord would put his Spirit on them!" Then Moses and the elders of Israel returned to the camp.*

Do you think that Moses just pulled that out of his head? Remember, that God's Holy Spirit was working in Moses. It was God giving a sign of what was going to be. That is the new relationship that Christ would initiate. It also would end up being the fulfillment of prophecies to come. *Jeremiah 31: 33-34, But this is the covenant that I will make with the house of Israel after those days, says the Lord: I will put My law in their minds, and write it on their hearts; and I will be their God, and they shall be My people. No more shall every man teach his neighbor, and every man his brother, saying, 'Know the Lord,' for they all shall know Me, from the least of them to the greatest of them, says the Lord. For I will forgive their iniquity, and their sin I will remember no more."*

In addition to the close intimate relationship, that God was going to establish, He was going to provide a new relationship of forgiveness toward man. He was going to put in a guaranteed forgiveness system not dependent on man's ability to avoid sin, but completely on His grace and mercy based on His unfailing love for mankind's soul. As seen above in Jeremiah's statement, God said He will forgive our iniquity and our sin and will no longer remember. However, the guarantee would be dependent on our belief in God loving us enough to send His Son to die for us. When we arrive to the New Testament we will find in the third chapter of John and the sixteenth verse a summation of God's plan. *John 3:16, "For God so loved the world that he gave his one and only Son, that whoever believes in him shall not perish but have eternal life."*

God's Nation Grows

Even after the nation of Israel embraced God's laws, they still did not understand that God desired much more from them than they were giving. They knew the law and were able to quote the law and impose the ritualistic practices and requirements of the law, but that was as far as it went for many of the religious leaders. The main component that God desired from them was missing. They did not understand the depth of God's love for them and all of His created people. Christ's coming would bring a new message and reveal a new kind of relationship with God. It would be the beginning of what God said earlier through Moses' desire that all believers would be filled with God's Holy Spirit and what later would be prophesied through Jeremiah 31: 33-34.

Later as the nation of Israel developed, God gave the people Judges to lead them but the people wanted a King. So God gave the people kings, and He continued to give them prophets to help guide the kings. Throughout the growth period, the prophets warned them, and the people, of impending judgement because of their disobedience but also prophesized God's deliverance because of His love for them. The process continued for centuries but by the time Christ would come, over four hundred years would pass since the last recorded prophet had come to the nation of Israel. However, Israel still would not understand the essence of God's teaching. They would know the laws of God, but they would not know God in the intimate manner God would desire. There would still be a need for man to continue learning the lesson that God desired and planned for man to know.

The time was now at hand to bring about the promise that He had made earlier and bring the people a redeemer. We will find that as far as the people were concerned, when God sent Him, He was not what they had expected and they refused to accept or believe that He was the promised Messiah. They would still have to learn the lesson of love that God wanted them to learn and more importantly, the lesson of love that God had for mankind's soul. They would only be concerned about the life they lived on earth and not their eternal existence. Christ was coming to let mankind know that their souls' eternal existence with Him is God's concern. God was about to bring His ultimate plan of salvation to fruition through the gift of His only Son. He had laid the foundation and had given hints along the way. He again would allow the stage of the deliverer of the people to be set by the killing of babies by a ruler trying to prohibit His plan. Again, the ruler would fail. Again, God would perform parting of a barrier in order that His chosen people could pass through to the other side. However, this barrier would not be a natural barrier, but a spiritual barrier. He would tear down the barrier of our sin to allow our souls to return home to Him and He could once again see them holy and blameless cleansed by the blood of Christ.

Chapter VI

OLD TO THE NEW

Father, forgive them, for they know not what they do

The primary goal for writing this book was to examine the statement that Jesus made at His crucifixion to His father, asking for forgiveness. Most think the statement was for those at the cross who were acting without the full knowledge and understanding of their actions. However, I believe differently. To get a deeper understanding of this statement, I believe we must look back to Adam and Eve. There, I believe we will find the real meaning of this statement. However the beginning of this statement, I believe, started before Adam and Eve. That is why I started our discussion from before God created the world in order to try to develop a pathway to understanding why Christ was on the cross to understand what the statement, I believe, really meant.

During the discussion, I attempted to develop some key background information to support the idea that the story of salvation started prior to the creation and that it started out of God's love for our souls. In doing so, I tried to show that when the scriptures I used from Ephesians were interpreted literally, they support the belief that souls existed with God prior to the creation. In addition to that, they also show that the souls were there because they were created through the God head entity, Jesus Christ, to be holy and blameless in the sight of God. In conjunction with Ephesians, I used Jeremiah and the Gospel of John as support. The scriptures I used are found near the beginning of the three books above.

After the discussion, on prior to creation, we moved to the beginning of the creation with a discussion about Adam and Eve. There we talked about the purity of Adam's and Eve's souls prior to their sin. We attempted, in a limited way to tie it to the characteristics of their souls prior to the creation and their actions after creation. We did this in an attempt to help understand the rationale of Adam's and Eve's act of disobedience, and what conclusions we could arrive upon from a closer examination of Scripture relating to their actions. This led into discussing God's initial relationship that mankind's soul and mankind had with God and the loss of that relationship. We attempted to develop a basis to show that the beginning of insight into Christ's statement on the Cross started in the story of Adam and Eve. Then we looked at some early indication of Christ shortly after the fall. We followed God as He continued to develop a deeper relationship with mankind and a road map for man to follow to arrive at His ultimate redemption of the souls He had always loved. We followed His creation and development of His people through the creation of the nation of Israel. We saw how Israel's relationship ran hot and cold toward God, and how God maintained a steadfast love for the nation.

We have finally arrived to the coming of Christ. As we approach the coming of Christ, we have already discussed some similarities in circumstances leading up to His coming. We did not mention them at the time but if we reflect back to Moses, we will see how a ruler tried to stop God's plan of Moses' birth by killing new born babies. Although the ruler at the time was not specifically targeting Moses, there is a similarity. In addition to this, we know God used Moses to part a barrier to deliver the Israelites from Pharaoh. God used His Son to part the spiritual barrier created by sin that separated us all from Him. We will move further into this discussion as we continue. However, before we do, let's look more closely at how God brought about Christ's birth and introduced Christ to mankind and see if we can decipher some meanings from this.

Zechariah & Elizabeth

We will use the Gospel of Luke to start the discussion.

Luke 1:5-7 In the time of Herod king of Judea there was a priest named Zechariah, who belonged to the priestly division of Abijah; his wife Elizabeth was also a descendant of Aaron. Both of them were righteous in the sight of God, observing all the Lord's commands and decrees blamelessly. But they were childless because Elizabeth was not able to conceive, and they were both very old.

In Luke we find the story of the birth of John the Baptist. Later Luke says that John the Baptist is the fulfillment of the prophecy by Isaiah 40:3. *Luke 3:4-6 As it is written in the book of the words of Isaiah the prophet: "A voice of one calling in the wilderness, 'Prepare the way for the Lord, make straight paths for him. Every valley shall be filled in, every mountain and hill made low. The crooked roads shall become straight, the rough ways smooth. And all people will see God's salvation."*

In the story of John the Baptist we can see right away a continuation of God bringing His plan to fruition. We first see a situation beginning similar to what started out with Abram and Sarai. We see two old people without a child, but they desire one. We find out that they both are righteous in the sight of God. It seems as if God setups situations where He can step in and bring about a miracle in order that it will help mankind understand better who He is and know His awesome power. The story continues and we learn from the story that Zechariah gets a visit from an angel who delivers him a message that He will have a son, and the son will be anointed with the Holy Spirit before he is born and will be great in the eyes of many. Again we see doubt arise. Because of Zechariah's doubt, he is told that he would not be able to speak until John is born. Later after Zechariah returned home, Elizabeth became pregnant with John.

So we are introduced to God's direct intervention again, after four hundred years of quietness. So from learning from God actions in the past, we can expect that He is preparing the way for something even bigger to happen. From what He did in the past; we know that he brought about deliverance after preparing the right conditions. The deliverance for the children of Israel came four hundred years after He first started the process with Abram. So we can expect deliverance is about to happen since God had waited four hundred years before.

This time the people really did not realize that they were in bondage. They did not know that they were slaves to their own misguided understanding of religion. They thought they were keeping the law that God had given them and did not understand that they were in need of a savior. However, God knew that they were still in need of a savior to save them from themselves. They were ignorant to the fact that they were dead due to sin and were helpless to do anything about it. God was about to save them from their ignorance. So let's continue to see how God's plan progressed.

Joseph & Mary

Long ago, God had His prophets tell the story of what He was going to do. Although they had told the story, it was not understood or believed. Here is one of the prophecies of Isaiah about the story we are about to look at and we will look at others as we continue. *Isaiah 7:14. Therefore the Lord himself will give you a sign: The virgin will conceive and give birth to a son, and will call him Immanuel.*

Mary

We begin the story about the fulfilment of this prophecy and the continuation of God's plan for mankind's souls with Mary and a visit.

Luke 1:26-33. In the sixth month of Elizabeth's pregnancy, God sent the angel Gabriel to Nazareth, a town in Galilee, to a virgin pledged to be married to a man named Joseph, a descendant of David. The virgin's name was Mary. The angel went to her and said, "Greetings, you who are highly favored! The Lord is with you. Mary was greatly troubled at his words and wondered what kind of greeting this might be. But the angel said to her, "Do not be afraid, Mary; you have found favor with God. You will conceive and give birth to a son, and you are to call him Jesus. He will be great and will be called the Son of the Most High. The Lord God will give him the throne of his father David, and he will reign over Jacob's descendants forever; his kingdom will never end."

From our reading, we find that Mary was visited by Gabriel an angel of God and given the message she was going to have a son and who the son would be. Of course, Mary was perplexed. She wanted to know just how that was going to be, since she was a virgin.

If we examine this story a little closer, we get a deeper appreciation of how God had been fulfilling His plan of redemption of mankind's souls. Remember, how we looked at the events that took place immediately after God told Adam not to eat from the tree of the knowledge of good and evil. We pointed out that after telling Adam this, God immediately created the suitable helper for Adam, who was Eve. Then the suitable helper enticed Adam to do what God had just told him not to do prior to her creation. He did and brought about the consequence of spiritual death. Now, in Luke, we find God using man's suitable helper, womankind, to bring His son into the world to reverse the consequence of the suitable helper's initial act of disobedience. How God uses the downtrodden and then elevate them for doing His work is a recurring theme in the Bible. This theme really sums up the story of the Bible and the lesson that God wants us to learn. It is the lesson of ultimate love. The lesson is that we must love those that are considered to be at the bottom. Although God gave example of this concept throughout the Bible, the ultimate example was the gift of His Son. Although He was and is greater than all, He humbled himself to be beaten and crucified for the lowest of us. God continued the illustration of love by establishing *"forever forgiveness"* through the death and resurrection of His son for those who believe in Him. So, no matter how undeserving womankind might have appeared and was viewed by man as being the catalyst for bringing sin into the world, God showed love for womankind and what a suitable helper she really was by using her to begin the fulfillment of the curse of Satan in *Genesis 3:15. And I will put enmity between you and the woman, and between your offspring and hers; he will crush your head, and you will strike his heel." One could interpret this as woman playing the leading role in God's plan of salvation of souls.* This act of forgiveness, should illustrate to all the ultimate act of love that God has for all by using a broken vessel to bring forgiveness through Christ to all.

After Mary's visit from the angel, Mary went to visit Elizabeth because the angel had told her about Elizabeth who was to bear a child in her old age. The Scripture doesn't say why she went to visit Elizabeth, but perhaps it was just to confirm what the angel had told her. If that was the reason, she received her confirmation immediately on approaching Elizabeth. As soon as Elizabeth greeted her, Elizabeth's baby who was in her womb leaped for joy and Elizabeth was filled with the Holy Spirit.

Luke 1:42-45. In a loud voice she exclaimed, "Blessed are you among women, and blessed is the child you will bear! But why am I so favored, that the mother of my Lord should come to me? As soon as the sound of your greeting reached my ears, the baby in my womb leaped for joy. Blessed is she who has believed that the Lord would fulfill his promises to her!" This must have been a confirmation to Mary of what miraculous thing was about to occur to her and for all mankind.

However, before the purpose of the birth was to occur, God had more teaching that He knew that man needed in order to begin to learn the lesson that He wanted them to know. Before the teaching came to its initial climax, several things would have to occur to further illustrate to mankind the significance of what was about to occur. First, mankind had to be told that the prophecies of the messiah were about to occur and then the birth would have to occur in a manner to fulfill scriptures. Then after the birth, opposition had to develop toward Christ for further fulfilment of scripture.

All of this was the beginning of the end of the covenant that God had made with Abraham, Isaac and Jacob. In addition, it was a pivotal point in the finalization of the curse in the garden that God had placed on Satan who was represented by Serpent. His head was about to be crushed. To get a deeper understanding of the crushing of the Serpent's head, we will look at what was brought about by the act of disobedience by Satan's temptation in the garden and then show the relationship of Christ's death and resurrection to it. We have mentioned it before in our discussions, but we will revisit it as we approach the consummation of the purpose of our discussion. However for now, we will continue to look at events leading up to the cross.

The Birth of Jesus

We see God continuing to set up situations to fulfill the scriptures concerning His plan of salvation for man's souls. We just discussed the situation where God moved to fulfill Isaiah 7:14. *Isaiah 7:14 says:*

"Therefore the Lord himself will give you a sign: The virgin will be with child and will give birth to a son, and will call him Immanuel." The angel announced to Mary that although she was a virgin, she would be of child.

As we read Luke 2:4 we will see how another situation came about to fulfill Micah 5:2. Micah 5:2 says: *"But you, Bethlehem Ephrathah, though you are small among the clans of Judah, out of you will come for me one who will be ruler over Israel, whose origins are from of old, from ancient times."* In Luke 2:4 we read that Mary and Joseph traveled to Bethlehem for a census count. While there it came time for Mary to deliver. There in Bethlehem, Jesus was born fulfilling the prophecy of Micah 5:2. As we continue to look at the birth, life, death resurrection and aftermath of the resurrection, we will see even more clearer the message of His love that God was and still teaching to mankind.

We have discussed God announcing His son's birth to Mary. We also read in the Gospel of Luke that an angel of God announces the birth of Christ to shepherds and specifically tells them who Christ is and where to find Him. *Luke 2:11, "Today in the town of David a Savior has been born to you; he is the Messiah, the Lord." In addition to this message a host of angles delivered this message, "Glory to God in the highest heaven, and on earth peace to those on whom his favor rests."* This message is a very important lesson that we may fail to connect with experiences that we later see take place in scripture and we experience in our lives as Christians. Some scripture's examples are the stoning of Stephens, the faith and calmness of Paul as he went through persecution. Remember the peace Stephen exhibited at his stoning. Even in the Old Testament we get an image of Christ bringing peace and comfort. In the story of the three Hebrew boys in the fiery furnace, we read in *Daniel 3: 24-25; Then King Nebuchadnezzar was astonished; and he rose in haste and spoke, saying to his counselors, "Did we not cast three men bound into the midst of the fire?" They answered and said to the king, "True, O king." "Look!" he answered, "I see four men loose, walking in the midst of the fire; and they are not hurt, and the form of the fourth is like the Son of God."* Theologians have said that the fourth person was Christ.

Not only have we experienced Christ's peace in the scriptures, but in our own lives, when everything seems to be crumbling and falling apart, we have experienced unexplainable peace in the mist of our turmoil, troubles and tribulation. That is the message of peace the angelic host was delivering to all mankind; the peace that would come from *"Christ's favor"* that was made available to all who would believe and accept Him as savior.

The Life and Teaching of Jesus

The life and teaching of Jesus is found in the four Gospels which are the first four books of the New Testament. In three Gospels, Matthew, Mark, and Luke, known as synoptic Gospels, similar stories are found. Although each Gospel was written with a particular purpose in mind, they all tell about aspects of the life and ministry of Christ.

The Gospel of John

The Gospel of John connects Christ more to God and shows His divinity and His humanity more than the other Gospels. In addition, John emphasizes God's love for mankind. He shows that God loved mankind so much that He gave His only son for our salvation. Although each of the Gospels has different themes, they all come together to tell the one story of God's love for our souls and His plan of salvation for them. As we continue to the cross, we will continue to see the story develop and culminate at the cross. We will see the connection of the consequence of the beginning act that placed Christ on the cross to His removal of the consequence on the cross. We will clearly see why Christ's statement of forgiveness on the cross has a direct logical connection to the initial act of sin which brought death into the world. However, before we arrive at that point, we will continue to see God's teaching ministry explaining to mankind through His example of sacrifice what love is and how much He loves mankind's souls.

After Christ's birth, the next time He appears in scripture was as a twelve year old boy astonishing people in the temple after He was left behind accidentally by His parents. When His parents told Him they had been seeking him, He asked, *"Why did you seek Me? Did you not know that I must be about My Father's business?"* This is the first indication that scripture gives that Jesus was aware of His earthly mission and scripture doesn't mention Him again until He was about to begin His ministry. We will use the Gospel of John to pick up this story. The Gospel of John, in a sense, picks up the lesson that God had been teaching mankind all along. John begins the story of God's plan of redemption for mankind by first identifying who Jesus Christ is. He establishes His identity and His divinity at the very beginning of his book by identifying Christ with the beginning of existence of everything. Shortly afterward John establishes His purpose for coming. Let's examine some of the beginning verses in the Gospel of John.

All things made through Christ at the Beginning

John1:1-5 In the beginning was the Word, and the Word was with God, and the Word was God. He was with God in the beginning. Through him all things were made; without him nothing was made that has been made. In him was life, and that life was the light of all mankind. The light shines in the darkness, and the darkness has not overcome it.

The Word became Flesh

John 1:14-15, And the Word became flesh and dwelt among us, and we beheld His glory, the glory as of the only begotten of the Father, full of grace and truth. John bore witness of Him and cried out, saying, "This was He of whom I said, 'He who comes after me is preferred before me, for He was before me.'"

John the Baptist Testifies he is not the Messiah

John 1: 19-27, Now this is the testimony of John, when the Jews sent priests and Levites from Jerusalem to ask him, "Who are you?" He confessed, and did not deny, but confessed, "I am not the Christ." And they asked him, "What then? Are you Elijah?" He said, "I am not." "Are you the Prophet?" And he answered, "No." Then they said to him, "Who are you, that we may give an answer to those who sent us? What do you say about yourself?" He said: "I am 'The voice of one crying in the wilderness: "Make straight the way of the Lord,"' as the prophet Isaiah said." Now those who were sent were from the Pharisees. And they asked him, saying, "Why then do you baptize if you are not the Christ, nor Elijah, nor the Prophet?" John answered them, saying, "I baptize with water, but there stands One among you whom you do not know. It is He who, coming after me, is preferred before me, whose sandal strap I am not worthy to loose."

Christ's Reason for Coming

John 1: 29-31, The next day John saw Jesus coming toward him and said, "Look, the Lamb of God, who takes away the sin of the world! This is the one I meant when I said, 'A man who comes after me has surpassed me because he was before me.' I myself did not know him, but the reason I came baptizing with water was that he might be revealed to Israel."

We can see from above, that John continued the teaching lesson of God's plan of salvation by initially identifying and establishing that in the very beginning, Christ existed and that all things were made through Him and ln Him was life and all mankind obtains light through Him. In other words, because He lives, we all *can* live if we accept His gift of life. John continued by showing the continuation of the teaching that God had begun in the Old Testament. He tells the beginning of Jesus ministry by starting with Christ's baptism by John the Baptist. By Christ starting His ministry in this fashion, He set an example for others to follow to indicate their acceptance of Him. In addition, it also shows the difference between what mankind can do and what God can do. John the Baptist baptized with water as an outward sign of belief, but Christ baptized with the Holy Spirit which brought about an inward change. This change is the lesson that God intended all along and still intends for mankind to learn. However, we will see as we continue to travel to the cross that the Jewish establishment failed to learn it as many of us have today.

John's Presentation of Jesus' Miracles

As we move into John's presentation of Christ's miracles, note how God led John to present them. They increase in relevancy to Christ's mission as He approaches the cross. His first miracle as we will see below had very little relevancy to His final actions on and after the cross. However His miracle of bringing Lazarus back from the dead was a defining statement about His power over death.

Jesus' First Miracle

We now come to Jesus' first miracle. In John 2 we read that Jesus was at a wedding and the wine had run out. Jesus' Mother came to Him and told him about it. There was some dialogue between Him and His mother that we will examine. I believe it makes a statement about God's plan. Part of the conversation we will examine follows: *John 2:3-4, "When the wine was gone, Jesus' mother said to him, "They have no more wine." "Woman, why do you involve me?" Jesus replied. "My hour has not yet come."* From Jesus statement, we see that Jesus is following a plan. The plan He is following is the plan that God made before He created the world.

After John tells about Jesus' first miracle, we read that Jesus is in the temple cleaning it. When asked about His authority to do such a thing and what signs can He provide, Jesus gave them the first direct indication of what was going to happen to Him, but they did not understand. *John 2:19, Jesus answered them, "Destroy this temple, and I will raise it again in three days."* They took it to mean the temple that was made by man. Later, in John chapter 3 we find Jesus talking to Nicodemus, and He again gives another indication. *John 3: 23-15, No one has ever gone into heaven except the one who came from heaven-the Son of Man Just as Moses lifted up the snake in the wilderness, so the Son of Man must be lifted up, that everyone who believes may have eternal life in him."* After saying this he continues to explain it in the familiar verses of John 3:16 and the following verses.

John Continues to Establish Who Jesus Is

As we continue to follow the Gospel of John, we will see John continuing establishing who Jesus is in part by quoting John the Baptist who was sent to testify of whom Jesus was and is. As John presents John the Baptist's testimony, we see that the lesson of God's plan and who Jesus is becomes clearer and clearer.

In John 3:25-36 we find John making this point again through John the Baptist. He writes beginning at verse 25, *"An argument developed between some of John's disciples and a certain Jew over the matter of ceremonial washing. They came to John and said to him, "Rabbi, that man who was with you on the other side of the Jordan- the one you testified about look, he is baptizing, and everyone is going to him." To this John replied, "A person can receive only what is given them from heaven. You yourselves can testify that I said, 'I am not the Messiah but am sent ahead of him.' The bride belongs to the bridegroom. The friend who attends the bridegroom waits and listens for him, and is full of joy when he hears the bridegroom's voice. That joy is mine, and it is now complete. He must become greater; I must become less." The one who comes from above is above all; the one who is from the earth belongs to the earth, and speaks as one from the earth. The one who comes from heaven is above all. He testifies to what he has seen and heard, but no one accepts his testimony. Whoever has accepted it has certified that God is truthful. For the one whom God has sent speaks the words of God, for God gives the Spirit without limit. The Father loves the Son and has placed everything in his hands. Whoever believes in the Son has eternal life, but whoever rejects the Son will not see life, for God's wrath remains on them."*

God's Wrath remains on those who Reject the Son

We clearly see John the Baptist telling explicitly that Jesus is the Son of God and that He has the power to remove death and restore life. Note that John the Baptist said that God's wrath remains on them who reject the Son. This indicates that wrath had been placed on mankind and the result of that wrath was death, and Christ was the agent to remove the consequence of that wrath. This is an important point that we must note on our journey to the cross. We must remember when the wrath began. It began in the garden with Adam and Eve.

In addition, we see John the Baptist providing the example of meekness with a subservient attitude that all Christians should follow. John the Baptist said, *"He must become greater; I must become less."* This is the attitude we as Christian must always reflect.

John's Gospel Stresses that Christ is the Messiah

John, in his gospel, continued to stress that Christ was the Messiah. We find him doing it next through the story of Christ meeting the Samaritan woman at the well. In addition, we see in John's gospel, God is continuing the teaching of the plan He started before the creation. It was God's plan all along that He would offer salvation to all of humanity. We first saw this in the covenant with Abraham where God told him that he would be father of many nations. Now as we read John, we see Jesus for the first time reinforcing and reaffirming the covenant. He did this in three ways. The first way was by starting the initial conversation with a Samaritan. The second was starting it with a Samaritan **woman** and the third was His statement that John recorded in *John 4: 21-24, "Woman," Jesus replied, "believe me, a time is coming when you will worship the Father neither on this mountain nor in Jerusalem. You Samaritans worship what you do not know; we worship what we do know, for salvation is from the Jews. Yet a time is coming and has now come when the true worshipers will worship the Father in the Spirit and in truth, for they are the kind of worshipers the Father seeks. God is spirit, and his worshipers must worship in the Spirit and in truth."* Although Christ indicated that salvation originated from the Jews, but all who worship God in spirit and truth would be accepted by God because that is what He wanted. We see here in John, the ushering in of a new type of relationship with God.

John's Gospel Builds to Show Christ's Divinity

John continues in his gospel of building on the divinity of Jesus and showing Christ's divine powers. As we continue to read, we see that John moves to the healing ministry of Christ and find that Christ heals a royal official's son by only declaring that the boy will live. After that we find Christ again doing a healing by merely speaking. In John 5:2-8, we read the following: *Now there is in Jerusalem near the Sheep Gate a pool, which in Aramaic is called Bethesda and which is surrounded by five covered colonnades. Here a great number of disabled people used to lay-the blind, the lame, the paralyzed. One who was there had been an invalid for thirtyeight years. When Jesus saw him lying there and learned that he had been in this condition for a long time, he asked him, "Do you want to get well?" "Sir," the invalid replied, "I have no one to help me into the pool when the water is stirred. While I am trying to get in, someone else goes down ahead of me." Then Jesus said to him, "Get up! Pick up your mat and walk." At once the man was cured; he picked up his mat and walked.*

John shows the divinity of Christ and His divine power by showing that just His words could bring about healing. In this story, another thing stands out that we might miss in our reading. Christ asked the man a question? The man had to declare that he wanted to be healed. God wants each of us to make a similar choice. He wants us to choose to be healed from our sin of death before we are covered under His grace.

We further see how John continued showing His divinity as he wrote about the authority Christ had. John tells the story about the Jewish leaders asking Christ what authority He had to heal on the Sabbath. In answer to their question Jesus answered, in *John 5:17 "My Father is always at his work to this very day, and I too am working."* After some more dialogue with the Jewish leaders John again returned to the power of Christ's words and his authority by quoting Christ in *John 5:24-27. "Very truly I tell you, whoever hears my word and believes him who sent me has eternal life and will not be judged but has crossed over from death to life. Very truly I tell you, a time is coming and has now come when the dead will hear the voice of the Son of God and those who hear will live. For as the Father has life in himself, so he has granted the Son also to have life in himself. And he has given him authority to judge because he is the Son of Man.*

God Continued to Teach His Plan of Salvation through Christ

All of this was part of God's plan to provide teaching to mankind about His plan of salvation through Jesus Christ. Christ's interaction with the people at that time was to continue on the path to fulfill God's promise of salvation. Everything was being prepared for His defeat of the consequence of man's original disobedience to God. The inspired writings of Matthew, Mark, Luke and John are part of God's plan that we in future generation would have record and knowledge of who Christ was and is. The inspired writings in the Old Testament laid the foundation for Christ and provided a historical path to Him.

In addition, as we look back on them, we see that God is faithful to His word and fulfills his plans in His own time. From the writings of the Bible, we also see that God uses many different people and circumstances to carry out His plans even when they may not be aware that they are being used.

John Continued providing Proof in his Gospel of Who Christ Was

John in his gospel continued to provide proof of who Christ was by writing about different things that Christ did and said. John finally got to the main point of why Christ had come. He quoted Christ as he had done in the previous stories, but what he quoted Christ said in the following passages sums up Christ's purpose of coming. In John 6:44-51, he quoted what Christ told the crowd who was among the five thousand He had fed that had followed Him across the lake afterward. *"No one can come to me unless the Father who sent me draws them, and I will raise them up at the last day. It is written in the Prophets: 'They will all be taught by God. Everyone who has heard the Father and learned from him comes to me.* No one has seen the Father except the one who is from God; only he has seen the Father. Very truly I tell you, the one who believes has eternal life. I am the bread of life. Your ancestors ate the manna in the wilderness, yet they died. But here is the bread that comes down from heaven, which anyone may eat and not die. I am the living bread that came down from heaven. Whoever eats this bread will live forever. This bread is my flesh, which I will give for the life of the world."

One of the things that Christ said in the above section confirms one of the themes that I have been making throughout. It is that God had been teaching mankind who He was and His plan of salvation from the beginning. Although His chosen ones had not understood His message, but whosoever did were and still are drawn to Him. Christ made it clear, that everyone would be taught by God but only those who heard or hear his voice will come to Him. The other important message that Christ gave during this dialogue with the people was that he was going to die for them. However, they did not understand what He meant when He said, *"This bread is my flesh, which I will give for the life of the world"*.

In the passage we just read, note how John tied Christ to God's deliverance of the children of Israel from the Egyptians and at the same time showed how God's acts in the past were tied directly to His coming. He compared the mana God gave from heaven to save the lives of the Israelites, to Himself coming from heaven to save the souls of all mankind. John continued to tell stories of Christ's encounters with those who were healed and believed, and His encounter with the Jewish leaders who rejected His teaching and sought to do Him harm. One of the miracles that John tells about was the healing of the man born blind from birth and later the story of Christ's conversation with the Jewish leaders on spiritual blindness. The remarkable thing about the story of the man born blind is that it set a background for the story that later followed. It's possible that John did not realize the relationship even though he wrote them.

After John tells about the healing of the man born blind, he finally arrived to where Christ talked about spiritual blindness and the consequence of it. This dialogue that Christ had with the Jewish leaders in the following passages in John 9: 35-41 sums up the Jewish leaders and also mankind's condition in relationship to seeing and understanding God's plan of salvation.

John 9:35-41. Jesus heard that they had thrown him out, and when he found him, he said, "Do you believe in the Son of Man?" "Who is he, sir?" the man asked. "Tell me so that I may believe in him." Jesus said, "You have now seen him; in fact, he is the one speaking with you." Then the man said, "Lord, I believe," and he worshiped him. Jesus said, "For judgment I have come into this world, so that the blind will see and those who see will become blind." Some Pharisees who were with him heard him say this and asked, "What? Are we blind too?" Jesus said, "If you were blind, you would not be guilty of sin; but now that you claim you can see, your guilt remains.

John did tie the two together in one sense by telling about the questioning of the man by the Jewish leaders and being thrown out because the man lectured them about God and Jesus relationship. Yet another aspect of the relationship between the story of Christ healing the man born blind and the dialogue with the Jewish leaders may not be apparent to some. So let's look at them more closely in relationship to the whole story of the Bible.

When we consider that we all are born spiritually blind in terms of needing to be saved from death brought about by the original sin, in view of the last statement in the dialogue above, we see a deeper connection between the two stories. They are not just about the Jewish leaders, they are about all mankind. The last statement by Christ, I believe, also plays a relevant part in the explanation of the forgiveness statement Christ made on the cross. We will attempt to bring together all the pieces of the discussions that have been pointed out as relevant pieces of the explanation to Christ's forgiveness statement when we get to the cross.

As John continues in chapter ten, we see him telling how Christ increased in teaching and laying out God's plan of salvation through Him. Yet the Jewish leaders and even His disciples had not come to understand. We see conflict continuing between the Jewish leaders and Jesus even to the point that they picked up stones to stone Him. However, Jesus escaped and went back across the Jordan and there got word of Lazarus' sickness and a request to go and heal him. Jesus delayed and Lazarus died. Lazarus was in Judea, where the Jewish leaders had tried to kill Him. When He told His disciples that He was going back to Judea they tried to stop Him because of the earlier actions against Him. Then He told them that He was going because Lazarus was dead and they followed him.

I am mentioning the story of Lazarus because it is following the progression that John has thus far used in showing who Christ was. As we have followed from chapter to chapter, we see how John's description of Christ's powers grows. We have seen Him turn water into wine; heal by His words a boy at a distance, and a man lane for thirty years. He has fed five thousand people with five loaves of bread and two small fish. He has walked on the water and healed a blind man. So we have seen Him show his powers over physical conditions and natural conditions.

In addition, we have seen Him though John's writings progressively tell those around Him who He is and what was going to happen to Him. That He was going to lay down His life and later pick it up. He told the Jews using their own history about who He was and that many of them would not accept Him, but He had other sheep not of the same sheep pen, that would follow Him.

Now we are about to see Him show his power over life and death through Lazarus' death. So Jesus went to Judea and as He had said, Lazarus was dead. Here we get a more personal glimpse of Jesus' compassion. Remember that Jesus knew that Lazarus was dead before He went and He had told His disciples that He had delayed for their benefit to help them to believe. So, Jesus knew that He was going to raise Lazarus from the dead, yet we read that *"Jesus wept"* because He was moved by the weeping of the others.

Here, we see how much love Christ had for humanity. Even though He knew that He was going to bring Lazarus back from the dead, He still wept because He felt the pain the others were experiencing. Looking at the bigger picture, Christ knew that He was going to give

His life for humanity. He must have had similar pain for all humanity because He knew there would still be many who would still suffer death because they would fail to believe that He was and is the Son of God.

As we continue to follow John's account of Jesus' actions, we arrive at Jesus calling forth Lazarus from the dead. When we look at the passage that John wrote to describe this event, we see the continuing theme of God's teaching of mankind about who He is and His plan of salvation for mankind through Christ. We read where Christ Himself makes this clear in *John 11:23-26. Jesus said to her, "Your brother will rise again." Martha answered, "I know he will rise again in the resurrection at the last day." Jesus said to her, "I am the resurrection and the life. The one who believes in me will live, even though they die; and whoever lives by believing in me will never die. Do you believe this?"*

Here Christ explains to Martha that whoever believes in Him will have eternal life. So we find God again using John to point this lesson out to mankind through the words of the one who provides life. Shortly after this, John describes the reason for the act that Christ was about to do to Lazarus. In John 11:41-42 we read, *'So they took away the stone. Then Jesus looked up and said, "Father, I thank you that you have heard me. I knew that you always hear me, but I said this for the benefit of the people standing here, that they may believe that you sent me."'*

We see again that Christ did it to help mankind understand that this was God's plan in action. The plan that we read about at the beginning in Ephesians talks about what God did before He created the world.

The Plan for Jesus' Death Increases

Now watch how God's hand is in the plan. After the miracle of Lazarus' return from the dead, there were some Jews who felt even more threatened in their positions. So a meeting of the Sanhedrin was called. Let's read the scripture as it was written and see how God uses us even when we may not be aware of it. *John 11:48-53, 'If we let him go on like this, everyone will believe in him, and then the Romans will come and take away both our temple and our nation." Then one of them, named Caiaphas, who was high priest that year, spoke up, "You know nothing at all! You do not realize that it is better for you that one man die for the people than that the whole nation perish." He did not say this on his own, but as high priest that year he prophesied that Jesus would die for the Jewish nation, and not only for that nation but also for the scattered children of God, to bring them together and make them one. So from that day on, they plotted to take his life.'*

Although the Jews were trying to keep people from believing in Christ, their actions actually caused more people to believe. They thought their actions were saving the Jewish nation, but God was using their actions to give all humanity the chance for salvation. So the Lamb of God's fate moved closer to the saving cross.

Shortly after this in John's gospel, we find the story of Mary anointing Jesus feet. This story set the stage for the introduction of Judas Iscariot and his money obsession. After this, John tells us about Jesus triumphal entry into Jerusalem on a donkey fulfilling the prophecy of Zechariah 9:9. The people's actions toward Christ as He entered Jerusalem on the donkey infuriated the Pharisees more. Jesus was aware that soon His hour would come and voiced it as the passages below indicate.

God continued to use John to write in a manner to teach mankind His plan. John did so by sharing Jesus own testimony showing that

He knew what His mission was and what was in store for Him and that He was willing to do God's will. Let's look at what John wrote in *John 12:23-33, 'Jesus replied, "The hour has come for the Son of Man to be glorified. Very truly I tell you, unless a kernel of wheat falls to the ground and dies, it remains only a single seed. But if it dies, it produces many seeds. Anyone who loves their life will lose it, while anyone who hates their life in this world will keep it for eternal life. Whoever serves me must follow me; and where I am, my servant also will be. My Father will honor the one who serves me. "Now my soul is troubled, and what shall I say? 'Father, save me from this hour'? No, it was for this very reason I came to this hour. Father, glorify your name!" Then a voice came from heaven, "I have glorified it, and will glorify it again." The crowd that was there and heard it said it had thundered; others said an angel had spoken to him. Jesus said, "This voice was for your benefit, not mine. Now is the time for judgment on this world; now the prince of this world will be driven out. And I, when I am lifted up from the earth, will draw all people to myself." He said this to show the kind of death he was going to die.'*

So we continue to see in John's Gospel, Christ's progression toward the cross. We see how Christ shared His fate with His disciples and others but they failed to understand His teaching. In a sense, it was the same teaching that God had given the prophets earlier to teach mankind about His plan of salvation and to prophesize how it would be carried out.

John continued the teaching by showing the divinity of Jesus through describing progressive miracles. By showing the divinity of Jesus, he showed that Christ was God's son. In addition, John showed the love that God had and has for mankind by showing the love Christ had for the ones that He loved. He did this by describing Jesus' weeping as Mary and Martha wept over Lazarus. John continued to show Christ teaching His disciples by describing Christ's feet washing of the disciples' feet. The significance of this teaching was that Christ wanted His disciples and His followers to demonstrate the same kind of love toward each other that He had for them. Because Christ knew that His actions would be recorded for future generations, He was also demonstrating how all of mankind should be toward each other.

Later John continued to show Christ's divinity and His knowledge of God's plan by describing Christ's remarks to His disciples concerning His death and betrayal. Christ demonstrated on previous occasions that God had shared His plan of salvation with mankind throughout. John showed Him doing it again in Christ's remarks that He was fulfilling scripture. We read that Christ quoted Psalm 41:9. *John 13:18 "I am not referring to all of you; I know those I have chosen. But this is to fulfill this passage of Scripture: 'He who shared my bread has turned against me.'"* This passage shows two things. The first is that Christ was the Messiah fulfilling prophecy and secondly, that He knew that He was going to be betrayed by Judas and it would lead to His death.

We also see another familiar pattern that Christ did that we also saw God doing in the Old Testament. Christ told what was going to happen prior to its happening in order to help mankind believe that He was who He said He was. We see this in the verse following John 13:18. John 13:19 *"I am telling you now before it happens, so that when it does happen you will believe that **I am who I am**.*

Even though we read the scripture, we sometimes pass over the connection that a verse makes with other verses in the Bible. This is one verse, I believe, we sometimes pass over without making a connection. Jesus is telling His disciple that He is the same God that called Moses at the burning bush that we read about in Exodus 3:14 which stated, *God said to Moses, "**I am who I am**. This is what you are to say to the Israelites: 'I am has sent me to you.'"* (NIV)

As Christ's time away from the cross shortened, we read in John, Christ explaining to the disciples in more detail about who He is.

Yet the disciples still appear not to understand. As John describes Christ's actions, one can almost feel the anxiety that Christ may have been experiencing. He had been teaching the disciples about His mission throughout His ministry, yet He was aware of their lack of understanding. Now, it seems that His teaching to the disciples intensified about the things that were to come after His death and resurrection.

Years of prophecies unfolded moment by moment as the cross grew nearer. Christ was betrayed by Judas, the soldiers arrested Christ and took him away. He was questioned by the high priest Caiaphas and later by Pilate. Pilate found no fault in Him, but as prophesized by *Isaiah 53:5*, *"… he was wounded for our transgressions, he was bruised for our iniquities: the chastisement of our peace was upon him; and with his stripes we are healed."* Pilate yielded to the wishes of the Jewish people and handed Christ over to them to be crucified. During this whole scenario, scripture was being fulfilled, but the Jews who should have known it, failed to see it through their blinded minds.

We have used the Gospel of John to follow the portion of Christ's life in the manner he presented it, in order to help illustrate the themes that the book has attempted to set throughout. From the very beginning we used the book of Ephesians to establish the theme that God loved mankind's souls so much that He created the plan of salvation for mankind's souls before He created the world. Because He created a plan of salvation for our souls before He created the world, we implied that it could indicate that He created the world to implement that plan. We again looked at Ephesians closer and zeroed in on one primary theme that is consistent throughout the Bible. The primary theme is that God loved and loves our souls so much. Because he does, God has always wanted us to know and understand how much He loves us and to understand how to love as He does. He loved us so much and wanted and wants us to understand the true meaning of love so much, that He sacrificed His son to help us learn that primary lesson.

What we have attempted throughout to show is that God started His lesson on love from the beginning and has maintained it throughout. We have also attempted to look at scripture and show a cohesive path from before the beginning of the world to Christ's birth, death, life, resurrection and thereafter. We have tried to do so by establishing a logical spiritual scriptural connection between mankind's souls and God before the creation of the world and after the creation. We did so by examining Ephesians through a nontraditional literal interpretation of its beginning verses. When we did, we saw that God's love for our souls were in existence before He made the world and interpreted that to mean that our souls were there with Him and He had a spiritual relationship with them. From this we developed a possible reason, driven by God's love for us, of why He may have created the world. That reason was because He loved our souls so much that He wanted to provide a temporary place where we could choose to spend eternity with Him instead of just being arbitrarily there. So, He created the world and mankind.

We then tried to show where the breakdown of that spiritual relationship occurred. From that point we began examining the spiritual rebirth of mankind and trying to understand through scripture the connection of mankind's fall to God's salvation.

Chapter VII

ARRIVING AT THE CROSS

Finally, we arrive at the cross where we will examine Christ's words of forgiveness on the cross to see if we can connect them scripturally and logically. Although we used the Gospel of John to arrive at Christ's crucifixion, His prayer of forgiveness is found only in the Gospel of Luke.

The Gospel of Luke not only provides us with the forgiveness statement of Christ; as we saw earlier, it also laid the foundation of the importance of one of the main characters we discussed in the Gospel of John. In Luke we found the story of the birth of John the Baptist. In John we saw the important role John the Baptist played in relationship to Christ. In studying the Gospels, we see how God used each of the writers to help tell the story of His plan of salvation.

As we examine the forgiveness statement, we will look at some of our earlier comments made about the statement and see if we can bring them all together to culminate our discussion. The first statements we will attempt to connect were made during the discussion in Genesis referring to Adam's and Eve's fall. We will start with the two entities mentioned.

The Tree of the Knowledge of Good and Evil and the Tree of Life

If you recall the discussion on the two trees found in the middle of the Garden of Eden, we talked about what Adam's and Eve's choice of eating from the *Tree of the Knowledge of Good and Evil* did for mankind. We saw that it took away life by bringing about sin and death, and how the *Tree of Life* gave or restored life. We mentioned that after the choice to eat from the *Tree of the Knowledge of Good and Evil, the Tree of Life* was blocked from Adam and Eve because of their actions. So how does the Tree of the Knowledge of Good and Evil and the Tree of Life connect to Christ on the cross. They connect through Adam's and Eve's actions.

Adam and Eve's Relationship to Christ on the Cross

I believe that most who are reading this already believe that Adam's and Eve's acts of disobedience brought sin into the world and as a result of their actions, Christ died on the Cross to reverse the effect. So, most already accept the fact that there is a relationship between Adam and Eve and Christ's death. However, I believe that the connection is also the genesis of the statement of forgiveness that Christ made on the cross. Let's examine why. We have discussed throughout about God teaching mankind who He was and is, and how He desired and desires mankind to know Him and know the love He has always had for our souls. But why did mankind need this lesson? To answer this question, we must look again to Adam and Eve. When we do, we recall that God forbade Adam to eat from the tree that gave him the knowledge of good and evil. However, Adam and Eve did so.

After Adam and Eve had eaten from the tree, remember we said that God, after talking with them about it, cursed the serpent, which represented Satan. We said that the curse was the prediction of Satan's defeat by Christ on the cross. In John, as we saw earlier, Christ validates that statement. John 12:31, Now is the time for judgment on this world; now the prince of this world will be driven out.

Not only did God curse the serpent, He blocked access to the Tree of Life that was in the Garden. Scripture tell us who the Tree of Life is. John 1:4 (NLT) says, *"The Word gave life to everything that was created, and his life brought light to everyone."* As we know from earlier verses in John that the Word is Christ. So what was the significance of the Tree of Life to Adam and Eve? The significance was that they always had access to it. They were always spiritually alive from having access to it. However, after their acts of disobedience, they no longer had access to it which cut off access to it for all mankind. Christ death and resurrection restored that access to mankind.

In addition, as soon as they ate, they realized that they were naked. As we discussed earlier, the awareness of their nakedness was a sign that they had lost a covering that they previously had. We said that it was the loss of God's Holy Spirit and the loss of eternal life. They died spiritually by blemishing the unblemished spiritual connection God had established with mankind through them. That was an important milestone in mankind's relationship with God. However, God's plan for mankind's salvation called for the blemished spiritual connection to be later unblemished. That's what Christ's death on the cross and His resurrection did for mankind. It opened up the channel to allow a pure unblemished spiritual connection to be made again with God. Through Christ's justification we could again in God's sight be holy and blameless. Let's look at some scripture to see if we can support this statement.

When Christ was here He told His disciples that after He departs, in other words, after He had removed the stain of death or the blemished spiritual connection brought on by the original sin, He would send an advocate that would be with them *forever*. *John 14:16-17 And*

I will ask the Father, and he will give you another advocate to help you and be with you forever- the Spirit of truth. The world cannot accept him, because it neither sees him nor knows him. But you know him, for he lives with you and will be in you. We know that it was the Holy Spirit. Christ's death and resurrection restored access to that covering and allowed removal of the feeling of nakedness for those who accept Him. Note that Christ said the advocate would be with them forever. That is insuring salvation because salvation is forever. In addition, He, the Holy Spirit, will live with and be in those who have accepted Christ. Again they will have continual access to the Tree of Life.

The Main Point

The connection with their loss of the Holy Spirit and Christ's restoration of it is a significant point, but that is not the main point that I am attempting to make here. The point is the question, "Why did they do what they did although God had told them the consequence?" I believe that the scriptures tell us. Although they tell us, we don't always see what they are saying because we are side tracked by traditional views and fail to use the power of the Holy Spirit to reason what they are saying. To me, the scriptures plainly say that God told Adam not to eat from the tree of the **Knowledge of Good and Evil.** Then it says when they did, their eyes were opened and they realized that they were naked. When I apply the logic of reasoning that God gave me while depending on the Holy Spirit guidance, it is clear to me that Adam and Eve did not know "good from evil" until they ate from the forbidden tree. I believe God was telling us that by naming the tree from which they were forbidden to eat. I also believe He specifically used that tree for the purpose for which He used it. Again reviewing what happened just after God forbade Adam to eat from the tree, He made him the suitable helper that enticed him to do so. I am not a preacher, but I see a sermon in that story.

The Whole Story

When we consider the whole story, I believe it points to the facts that their action was performed out of ignorance and brought about from the gift of freewill. Their action out of Ignorance brought death through sin into the world. Christ's action of death and resurrection over turned their action for those of us who believe that God loved us enough to send His Son to die for our redemption. Considering that they acted out of ignorance, I believe a nexus exists between Christ's statement of forgiveness on the cross and Adam's and Eve's actions in the garden.

I will paraphrase Christ's statement to make the connection clearer. *"Father forgive the act of the SIN that was performed out of ignorance that brought death to all mankind because when it was committed, they did not know it was evil because they did not know the difference between good and evil."* Note that I capitalized the word SIN; because Christ came to take away the SIN of the world, not the sins of the world. As we read in John 1:29, *The next day John saw Jesus coming toward him and said, "Look, the Lamb of God, who takes away the sin of the world!* Note that John the Baptist said the SIN of the world. So Christ's act on the cross removed the result of the sin of the world which was death.

In addition to considering Adam's and Eve's actions, there are other indications that add credence to my belief that Christ's statement on the cross had deeper ramifications toward mankind's acts of sin from ignorance. When we look at John 9:35-41 before, we said we would later tie in Christ's comments when the Pharisees asked, *"What? Are we blind too?"* and Jesus said, *"If you were blind, you would not be guilty of sin; but now that you claim you can see, your guilt remains.* Again considering the statement of Christ to the Pharisees, He was saying to them, since you claim that you have had your eyes opened to the spirit of truth, and you refuse to accept the spirit of truth that

I am offering, your guilt still and will remain. My death on the cross will have no meaning to you Pharisees and my prayer of forgiveness, for those who know not, will not apply to you because you claim that you already know.

It Is Finished

Later in John 19:30 we find Christ last words, *"It is finished."* God had just about fulfilled the promise that He had given Jeremiah to prophesize. The forgiveness part of Jeremiah's prophesy was complete and Christ's resurrection, ascension and coming of the Holy Spirit would setup the completion of the rest of it. *Jeremiah 31:33-34, "… I will put My law in their minds, and write it on their hearts; and I will be their God, and they shall be My people. No more shall every man teach his neighbor, and every man his brother, saying, 'Know the Lord,' for they all shall know Me, from the least of them to the greatest of them, says the Lord. For I will forgive their iniquity, and their* **sin** *I will remember no more.'"*

His mission of providing restoration of mankind's soul to an eternal state of existence with God was over. The **sin** that brought death to all would not be remembered any more for those who accept the gift that God gave – His Son.

When we consider that Christ's mission here was to provide salvation for mankind, it makes logical and scriptural sense to connect his final acts and prayer to that mission. It is befitting to believe that His prayer of forgiveness was for the sake of all mankind and if it were, the scenario in which I have presented makes it scripturally logical and scripturally plausible.

Christ's act on the cross was God offering proof to mankind of the depth of His love for our souls and also a lesson for mankind about how we should love one another. In spite of our failures to be obedient to Him, He still loved and loves us unconditionally. He sent His son to die for us while we were still sinners, so that we could make the ultimate choice to live with him forever. I don't only think it was all about just living with Him, I believe it also was about living a more connected and abundant eternal life with Him; an eternal life where our souls will be able to appreciate His love for us even more because they had experienced the opportunity to understand what it was like away from Him and to learn what love is.

John 10:9-10 I am the door. If anyone enters by Me, he will be saved, and will go in and out and find pasture. The thief does not come except to steal, and to kill, and to destroy. I have come that they may have life, and that they may have it more abundantly.

I pray that the grace of God abides with you, His love engulfs you and His mercy embraces you. Amen

I sit and I See

I see beyond that - that is before me.
I see from that - that was, that - that is.
I see from that - that is, that - that will be.

MOM

Experiences through the years have bestowed wisdom and given insight into life through the totality of her experiences. Witnessing many scientific and technological changes have destroyed, changed and developed new philosophical and theological thoughts. She sees. She sees much more than just the reality of that which is before her, she sees from that – that was, the past, and the totality of that – that is, the present. Like an intricate mathematical function the summation of each integral of that – that was and that – that is, provides sight into that – that will be, the future.

www.ingramcontent.com/pod-product-compliance
Lightning Source LLC
Chambersburg PA
CBHW051215120626
46547CB00013B/1364